Beloved

Zoe Leavitt
Counselling Psychologist

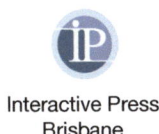

Interactive Press
Brisbane

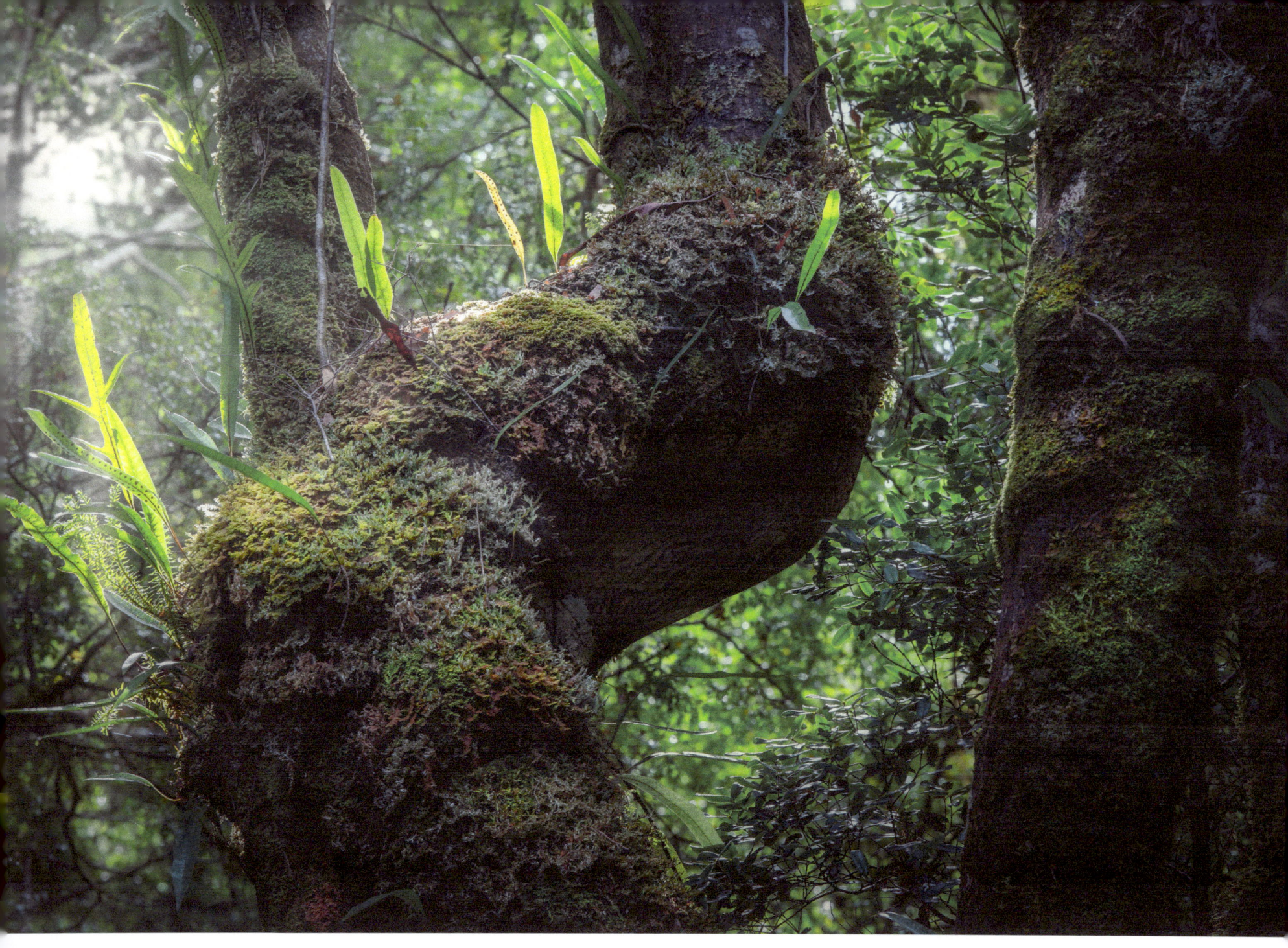
SAVAGE RIVER NATIONAL PARK

This book is dedicated to Roger Ballard

Thank you for giving me the diamond key
Which opened the door
And allowed my heart to return home.

for Yorgi, Elijah and Asha

My love for you is immeasurable.

May Breath be your Prayer
May Humanity be your Religion
May Consciousness be your God.

– author unknown

CONTENTS

    1. The Calling   3
    2. The River, the Ocean, and All In-Between   19
    3. Fear and Loss   31
    4. Longing and Devotion   35
    5. The Essence   55

PHOTOGRAPHS

SAVAGE RIVER NATIONAL PARK 11
SAVAGE RIVER NATIONAL PARK x
TRIAL HARBOUR 2
NELSON FALLS 4
TASMANIAN NORTHERN COAST 6
PIEMAN RIVER, CORINNA 10
CRADLE MOUNTAIN NATIONAL PARK 12
PRINCES SQUARE, LAUNCESTON 16
TARKINE/TAKAYNA FUNGI 20
SARAH ANNE ROCKS 24
CHURCH ROCK, ARTHUR RIVER 26
SUMAC LOOKOUT 30
LAKE PLIMSOLL 34
TAMAR RIVER, LAUNCESTON 36
SAVAGE RIVER NATIONAL PARK 40
MOUNT MURCHISON, TULLAH 42
NORTH-CENTRAL TASMANIA 44
NELSON BAY 46
CORINNA TARKINE/TAKAYNA 50

FARMLAND, LEBRINA 52
CENTRAL PLATEAU 54
LIFFEY FALLS 56
CRADLE MOUNTAIN NATIONAL PARK 58
DRONE IMAGE, WETLANDS, CYGNET 62
CRADLE MOUNTAIN 64
TRIAL HARBOUR 68
MACINTOSH DAM, TULLAH 70
LAKE ROSEBERY, TULLAH 74
COUTA ROCKS 76
CRADLE MOUNTAIN NATIONAL PARK 80
WEDGE-TAILED EAGLE, CORINNA 82
BINALONG BAY 86
LIFFEY RIVER 90
CYGNET WETLANDS 92

Acknowledgements

Thank you so much to David and all the team at Interactive Publications for the opportunity to work with you and publish this labour of love. Thank you also to my reviewers for all your support and your incredible reviews. Thank you for being so generous in your correspondence and so open to our connection; it hasn't gone unnoticed or unappreciated.

I would also like to pay particular homage to my husband and creative director, Craig George (Yorgi). Without your support this book would never have come to fruition. Thank you for your unwavering love and support, practical, emotional and creative. Thanks for putting up with my quirkiness; we are opposites in some ways, but we always find a place to meet. As I have told you, 'you feel like home'.

A special thank you to Asha and Eli for their love and support throughout this journey. I will be forever grateful.

I would like to thank my family, who have always stood in the wings and supported me throughout. I also feel very fortunate to have special friends, whom I cherish, scattered across this vast continent and overseas.

Finally, a very special acknowledgement to Dr Paul Holman. We are kindred spirits, and you have held my hand all the way.

Foreword

In one of William Blake's visionary art pieces we see an angel diving down from heaven blowing a trumpet. Wake up! You are lost in your slumber, dreaming your little fears and desires. Rouse yourself to vision, to reality and, as Blake would have it, to the Imagination!

In Zoe's work we are the beneficiaries of vision and inspiration; in her verses we hear Spirit speaking and "blowing where it listeth" (John 3:8 KJV Bible).

Thus there is only one question for us: "Can we be available to this message of the heart?" Can we drop our many stories and listen in a completely open way?

We are not alone in our search; Zoe reminds us of that good companion, the breath, whose ministrations lead us surely to that which we are seeking.

Please relax and enjoy this opportunity. This is no 'New Age' collection of self-help nostrums. These words come directly from That Which Sustains Us, whether we know it or not.

– Dr Paul Holman, Author of *Living Space: Openness and Freedom through Spatial Awareness* and *Hawks, Doves and other Humans: Discovering a New Science of Constitution, Temperament and Health*

Preface

I have always been a seeker, searching for a communion with my inner self, yet to also a transcendence, the dissolution of self, leading to a sense of the beauty inherent in us all. This led to a lot of soul searching from a young age. In 2000, I met a very special meditation teacher, Roger Ballard, who taught me the power held within vibration and thought. He changed my life by teaching me the importance, the absolute imperative, of training your mind.

This is my story but also yours. I hope it helps to draw you into your inner being, cultivating the alchemy needed to merge self and spirit. Inviting the magic of your soul to come forth, embracing humanity and nurturing the compassion we so desperately need.

This work acknowledges the feminine aspect of spirituality, which lives within us. She is to be celebrated: for too long, our wisdom and intuition has been diminished.

The photographs in this book are from Tasmania, especially the Tarkine Region, the largest sub-temperate rainforest in the Southern Hemisphere. It is sometimes called the 'Mother Forest', and there is no other place quite like it. It is steeped in mystery and ancient wisdom.

This book is intended to be read as you wish, in a meditative sense, for solace, comfort and reflection. To be picked up and opened when you feel the urge, to dip in and out of as needed. It is my soul calling to yours.

Prologue

In the beginning, Mother enveloped me, and I could feel her heartbeat within mine. Resonant and deep, she held me so and showed me the garden she was creating for me.

"Eve" she named me, for the source of life carried in my seed. She held me tenderly and placed me gently upon the Earth.

Into the garden I grew. Iridescent beauty blossomed all around. The air shimmered with vibration and radiance.

I came to a waterfall, and there I met Adam. I looked into his eyes and found my twin soul. Together, we embraced and all at once, I felt completely whole.

We loved our garden, we danced under the stars. We bowed to the moon and sun. We cared for the flowers and animals. We cared for One, our Mother, who held us all. Awareness flowed all around, through the trees, the flowers, the animals. A sentient web, connecting us all.

"I will call you Gaia," Mother pronounced. "I give you this garden, to love and behold; I give you my heart, I give you my soul."

In Gaia, we lived, and Mother we loved. Deep in our hearts, we felt her presence, luminous and alive. She lived through the flowers and the trees, and we felt her carried in our breath and in our seed.

One day, she gave me a mirror – a pool of the clearest light – to show me the beauty inherent in me.

I gazed lovingly within; I saw the lock before me and turned the key. I opened my heart to all she had given me.

I bow before her. Pray, let me not forget the power within my Divinity.

Let me return to the garden, help me break free.

I will tend to her with care, cast out the weeds, plant beautiful flowers and let you love me.

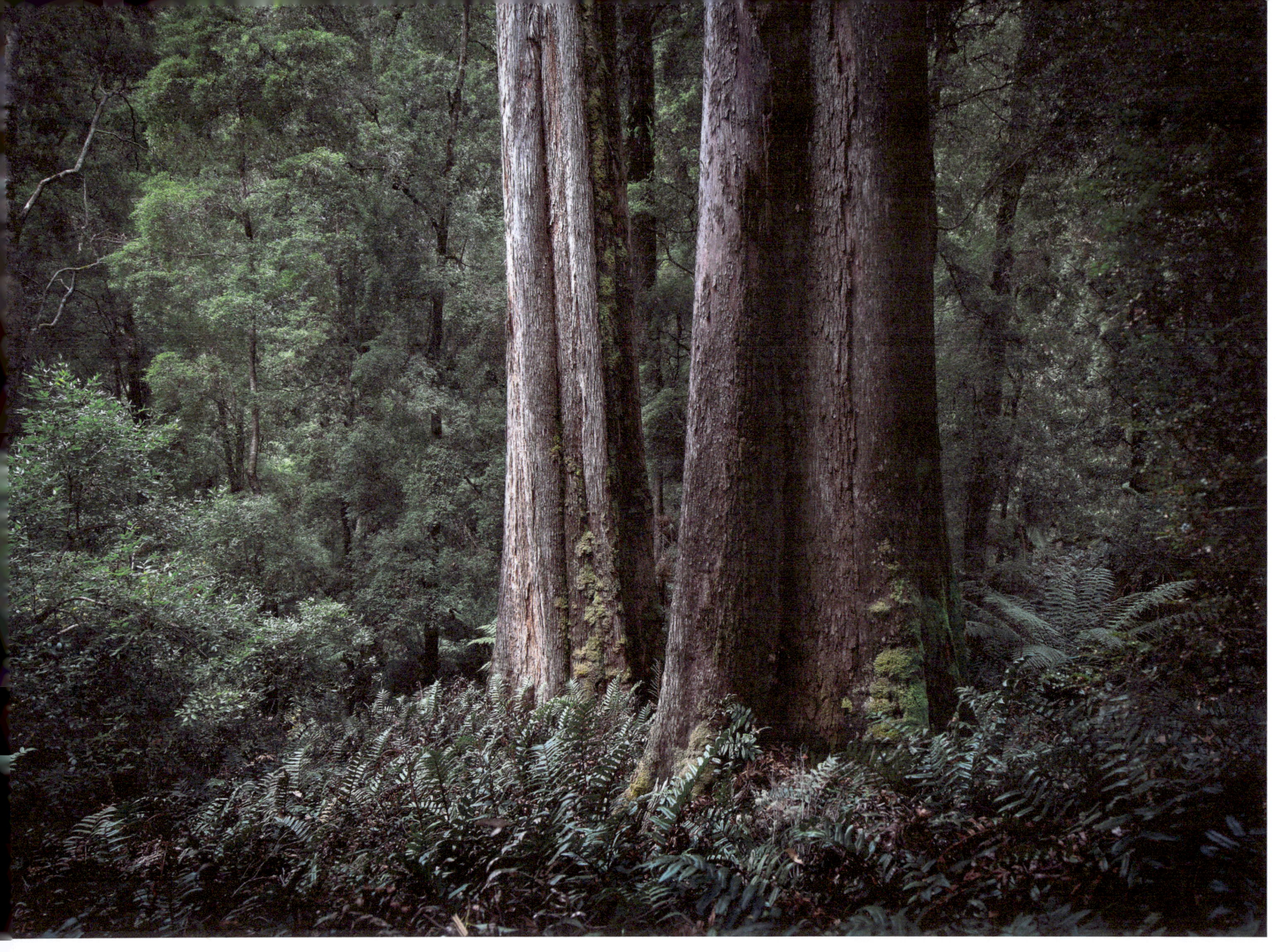
SAVAGE RIVER NATIONAL PARK

Rock me in my cradle
Awaken me from sleep

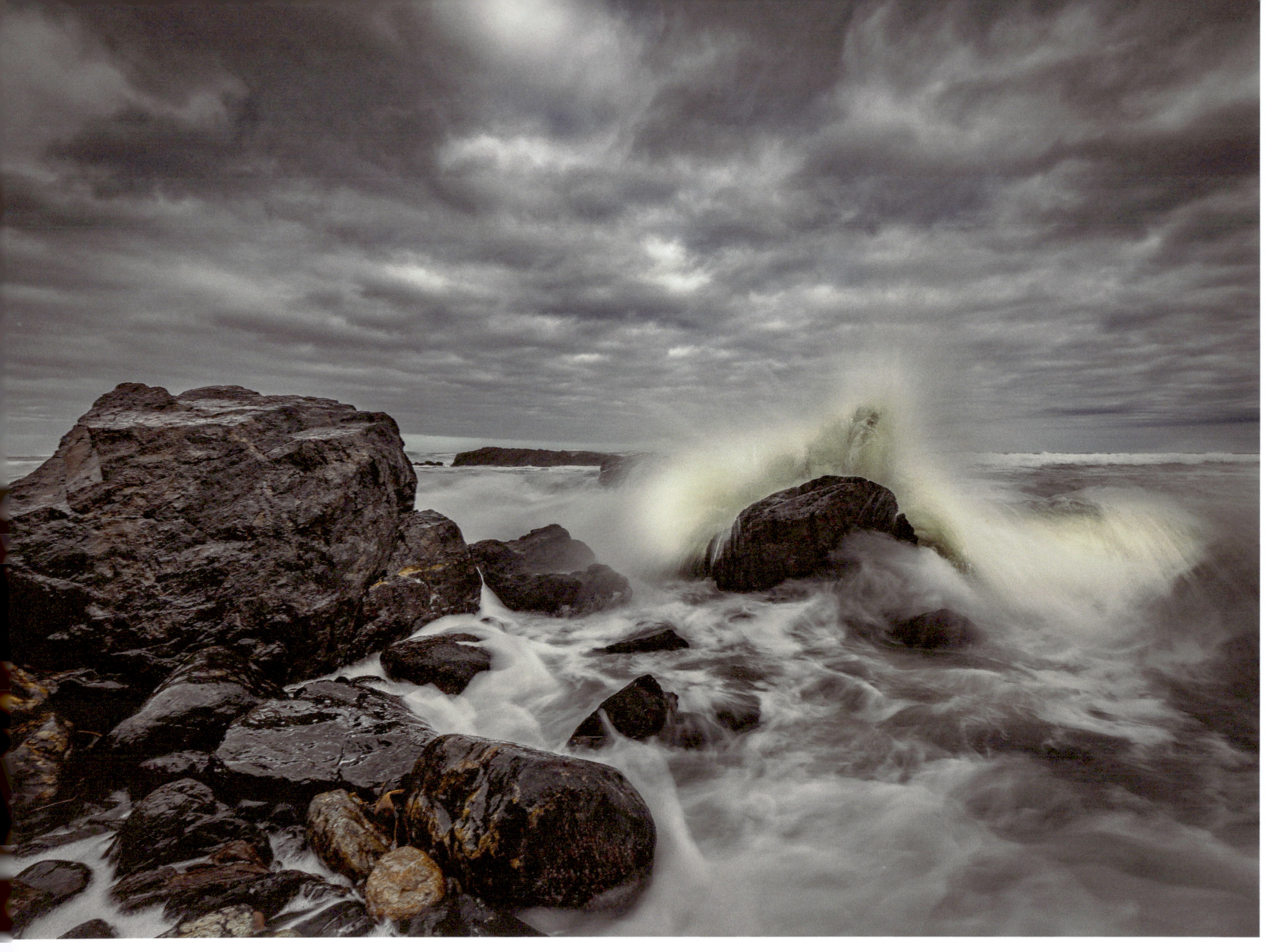

TRIAL HARBOUR

1.

The Calling

Faith is a knowledge within the heart, beyond the reach of proof.
– Khalil Gibran

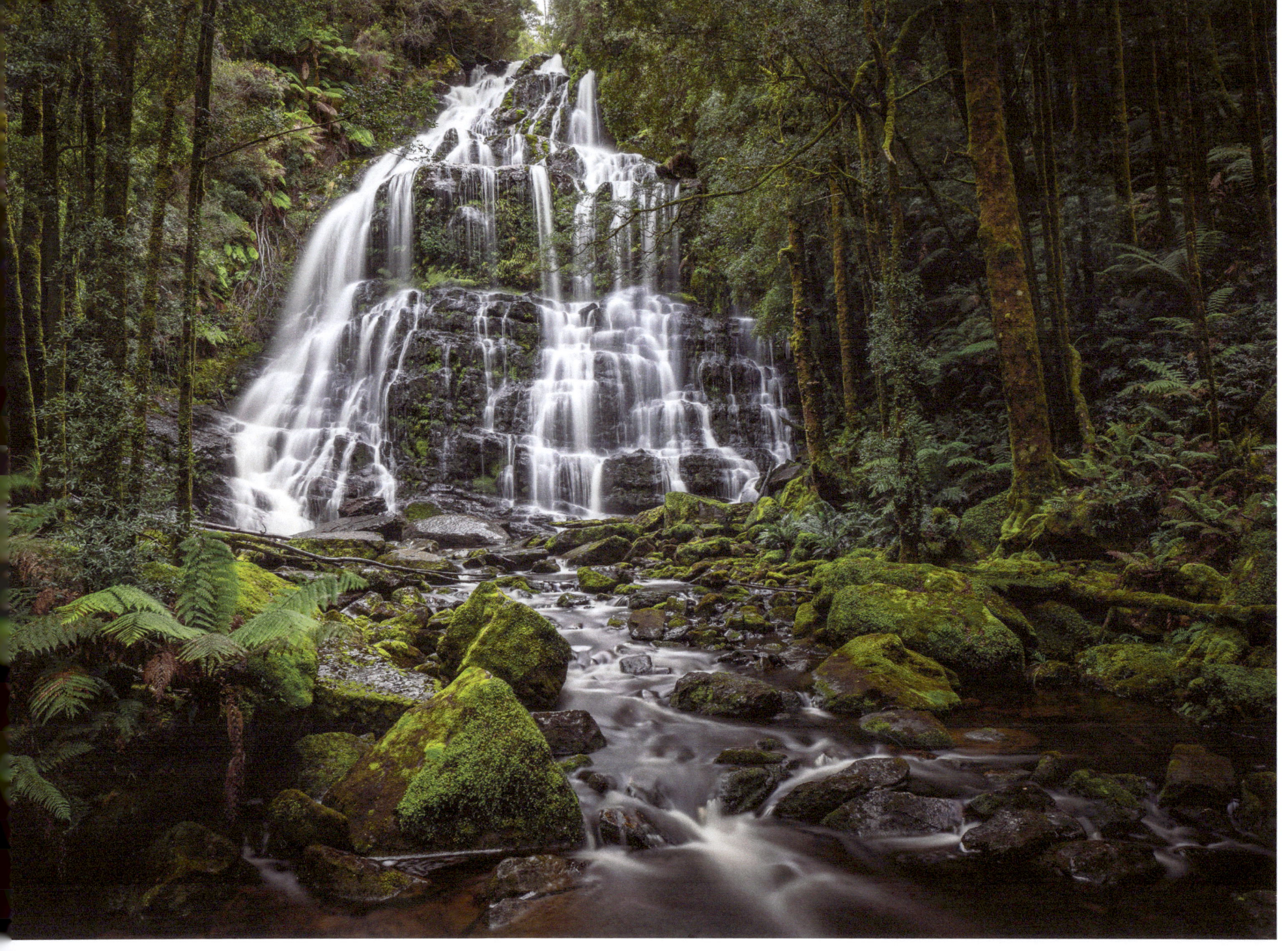

NELSON FALLS

Come to me
Open my heart
Let me drink

For when I bathe in your nectar
I realise I was dried up and shrivelled
Thirsty and raw

Crying for sustenance
But never finding the door

Do not look for me outside
Do not look within
Hoping for my treasure
The grasping makes the mountain higher

Rather

I am in the silence between your inhale and exhale
I am in the space beyond your mind
I am in the vibrant flow of your heart

Can you feel my pull?

I call you home

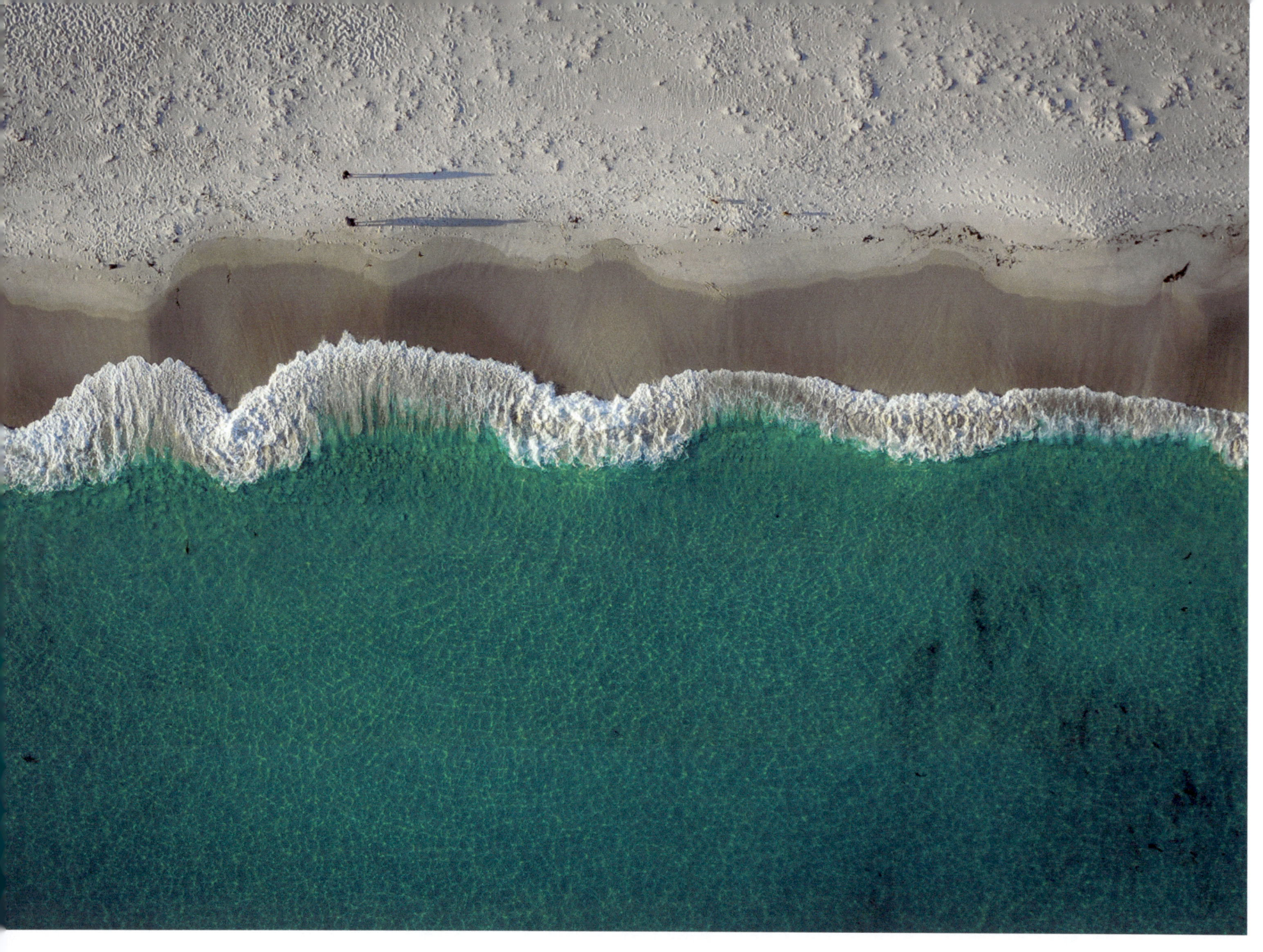

TASMANIAN NORTHERN COAST

I was so lost
All at sea
Until you came
For me

Live in my Garden
Be with me

Feel your luminescence
Grown from a seed

Enter me slowly
So that I may come to know you

Enter me with a rush
So that I may finally see

We stand bereft
At the banquet of life

Hollow
All at sea

Relinquish yourself

Be with me
Breathe in my ocean
Feel you
Within me

Surrender to me
I will hold your hand
I will carry your flame

Bow your head
Begin to understand

All that we are
All that is real
Lives in your heart
Where your soul is revealed

Be with me now
We have no time to waste
Let me carry your flame
May your soul awake

The call of the heart
Is not unlike the whale's

Steady and strong
Like a beat in the sea

So much more
Than just blood and muscle

But a beacon of light
To help me find me

Beloved

When will I know you?
When will I see?

When my breath becomes the ocean
And you find me

Our hearts intertwine
For all to see

For when I feel your caress
And I sink into bliss

I realise we were always
Meant to be

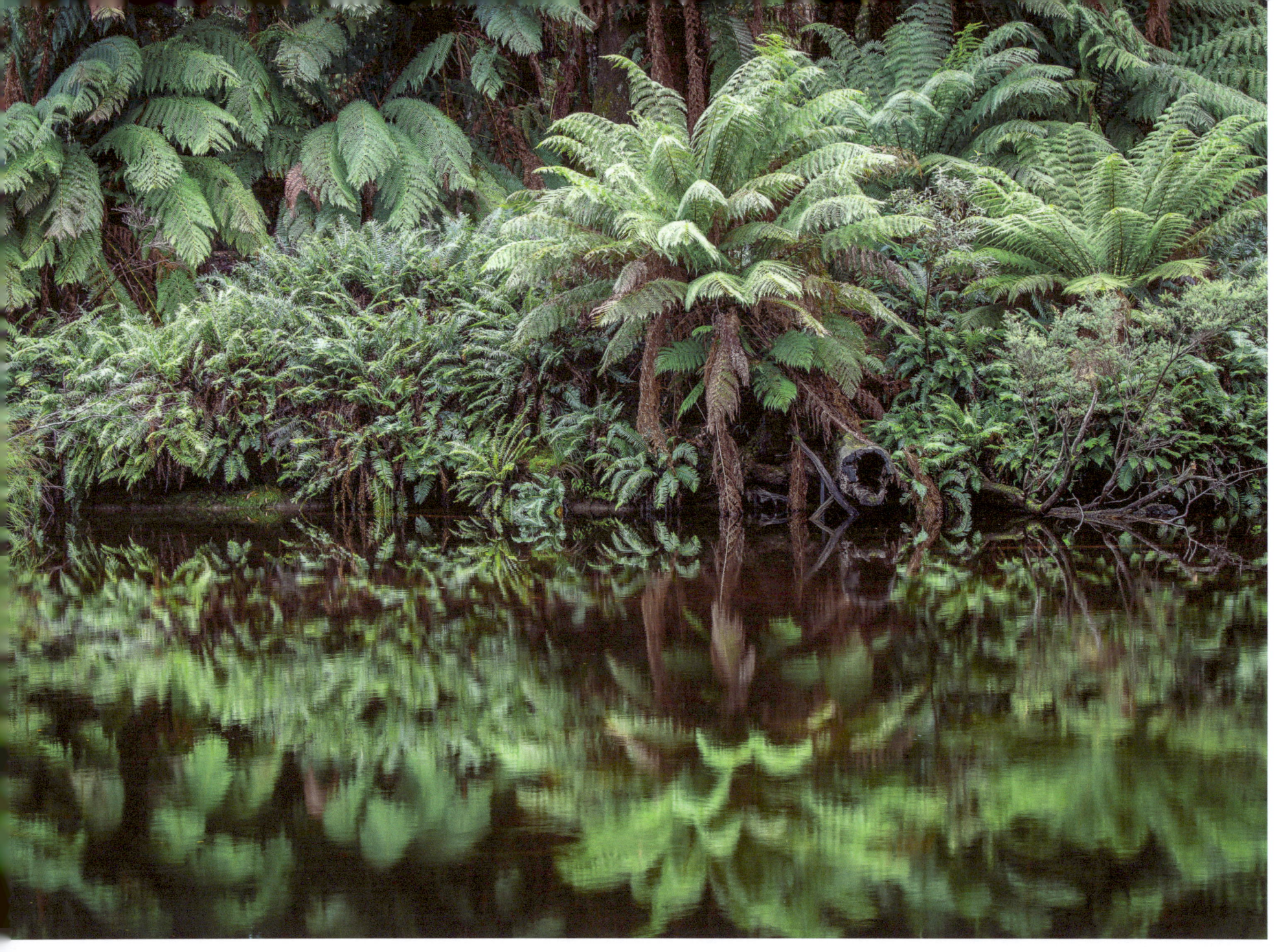

PIEMAN RIVER, CORINNA

Come to my garden
Feel my hallowed space
Inhale the sacred scents
Lie down beside me
So we can embrace

Come to my garden
Naked and raw
Feel the fire burn between us
As I open your door

Come to my garden
Allow my love to enfold you
Do not be afraid
Watch all the old dissolve
As you fall away

Come to my garden
Take my hand
And finally understand
All that you are
Exists in your heart

A seed or a flower
It doesn't matter
For we can never
Be apart

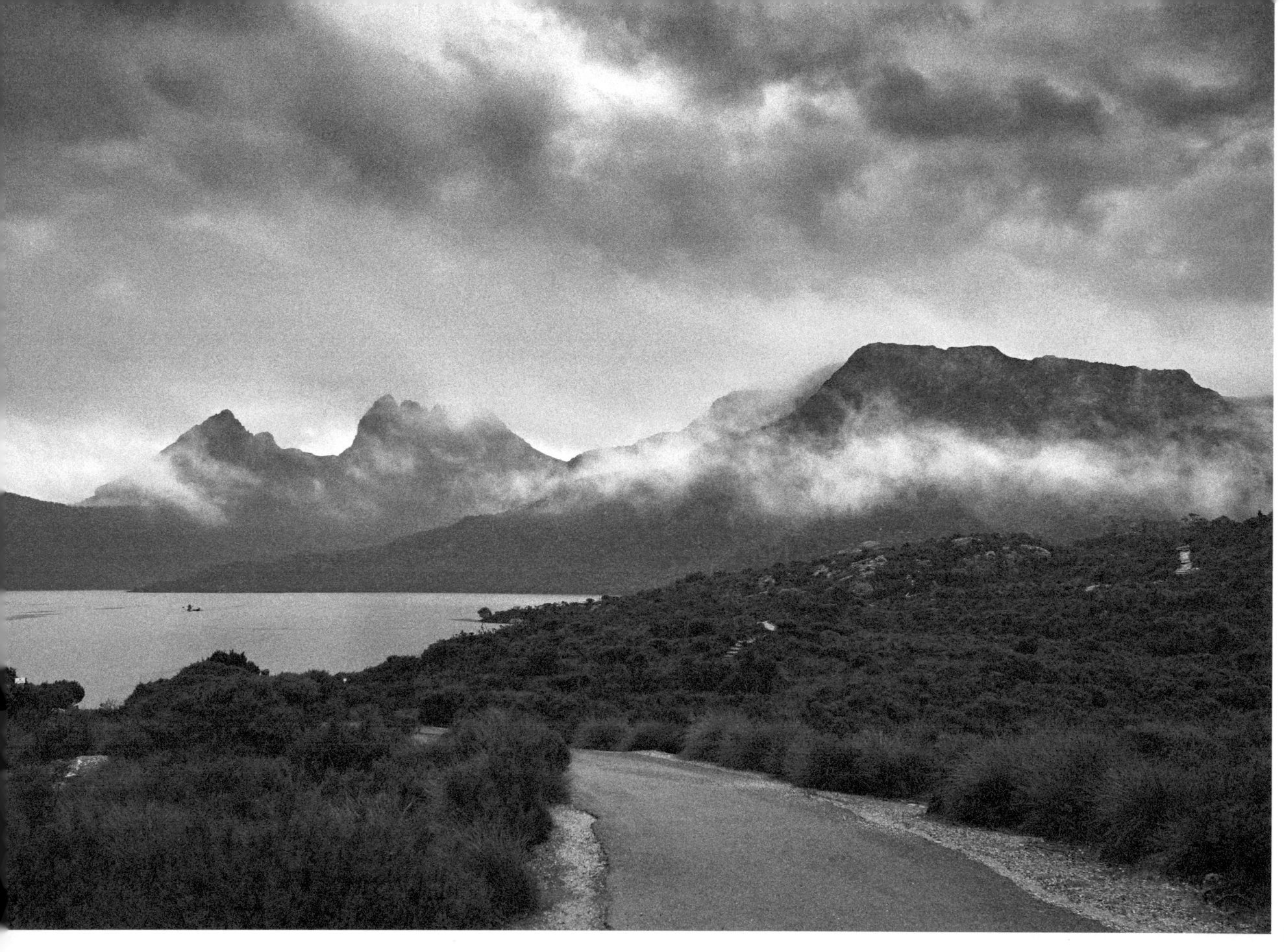
CRADLE MOUNTAIN NATIONAL PARK

Beloved

I feel your call

May I feast
Not on delicacies or wine
Not surrounded by treasure

Only sumptuous nourishment
Alms for the soul

As I bow within
Feeling my light unfold

Beloved

May I come to you holy
May I come to you clean
Not bloodied and broken

May I come to you
Resplendent and whole
In all I have forsaken
Turning dust into gold

May I come to you
My flower unfolding
Intertwined with me

My heart awakes
With the warmth of your touch

Then I realised
All that I was, before
Just a grain of sand

Now an indelible trace
A carving of love
A crystal, formed in your hand

Only a drop of nectar
Is needed

So you
Feel me

Take my hand
Be with me

Bow to the heavens
Whilst setting yourself free

Show me the key
And I will show you its lock

Show me the light
And I will show you its path

Show me your love
And I will show you Infinity

Show me yourself
And I will show you Divinity

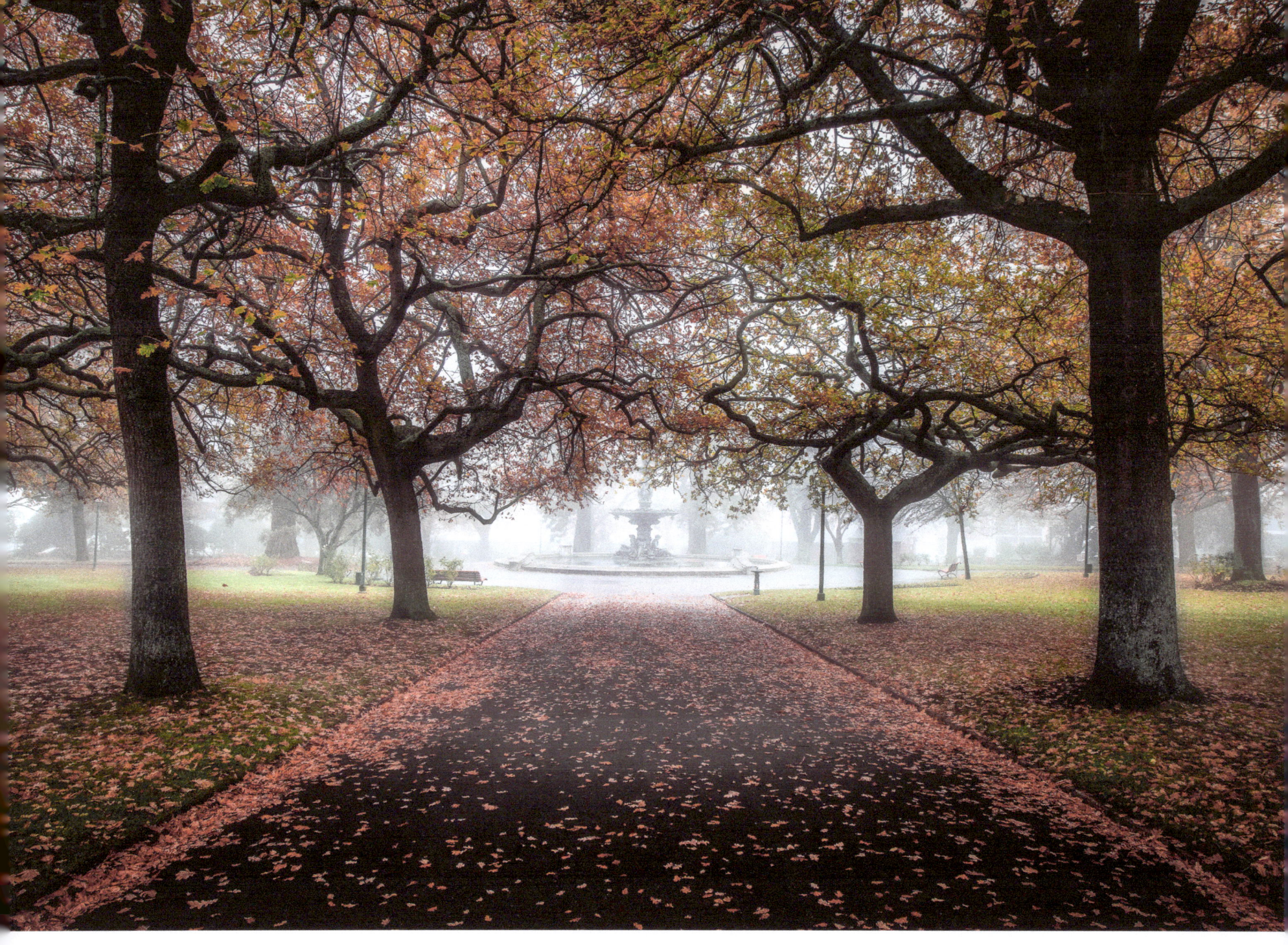
PRINCES SQUARE, LAUNCESTON

Can you see me?

Hold out your hands
Do you feel me?

Is love bleeding from your heart?
Are you spellbound?

You are not alone
I am always here

Take my hand
I will guide you

Soothing your pain
Washing your fears away

As I hold your hand
And your light unfolds

And I can finally
Stay

Come

Mark your course
By the stars and the trees

Feel the winds
Caress you with ease

Hold my hand
I will carry you

Gaze upon me
Feel your luminescence

Our hearts will find the way

Come to me broken
Or come to me whole
Come inside, out of the cold

May I wash your sorrows
Soothe your cares

Seek your epicentre
And find me here

Drink my love
Have your fill

Feel your heart overflow
Until all fear
Is finally still

2.

The River, the Ocean, and All In-Between

All that we are is the result of what we have thought.
– Buddha

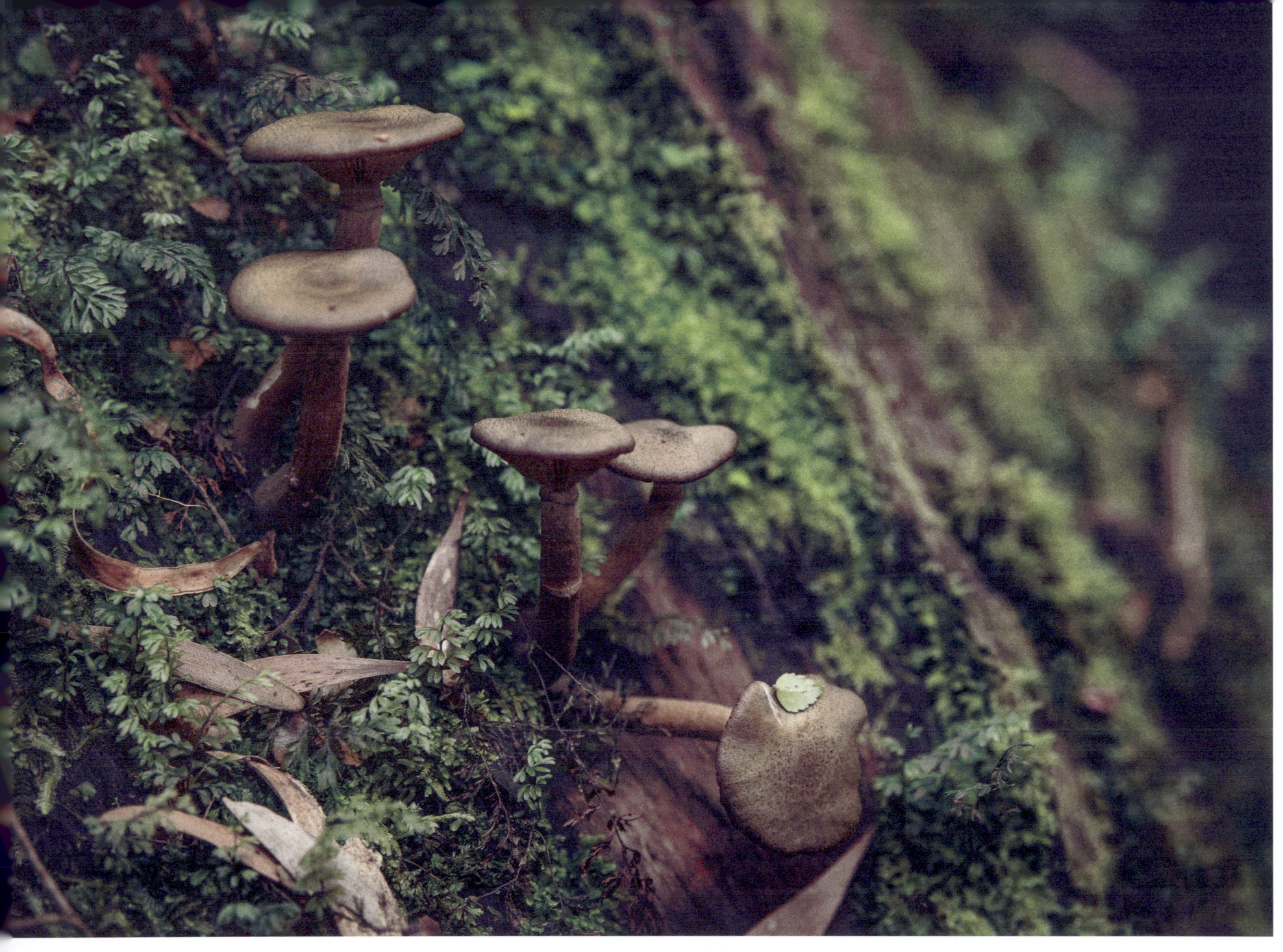

Breath is a river
To infinite bliss

Slip into the ocean
Flow into my love

As all that I am
Is held in your caress

Aaaah!

Just watching the breath
Some would say
Is a thing of beauty

Is it really just that?

Or is it not
The hand of the Divine
Reaching out
Inviting us to stay?

Freedom is facing things
Owning your fear

Shine a light on it
Allow it to fade

And disappear

So much suffering
So much pain

We can be free
Inhale
And truly breathe

Feel the river come alive
Feel yourself
Start to free

Feel the love
In your heart

Feel the love
Within me

It is freedom we seek
And love we crave

But it is in loving ourselves
That we become truly free

No one escapes the tyranny of time
The key is to dance with her

For when she holds you
And you feel the flow
You realise that in death is rebirth

To flow
We must let go

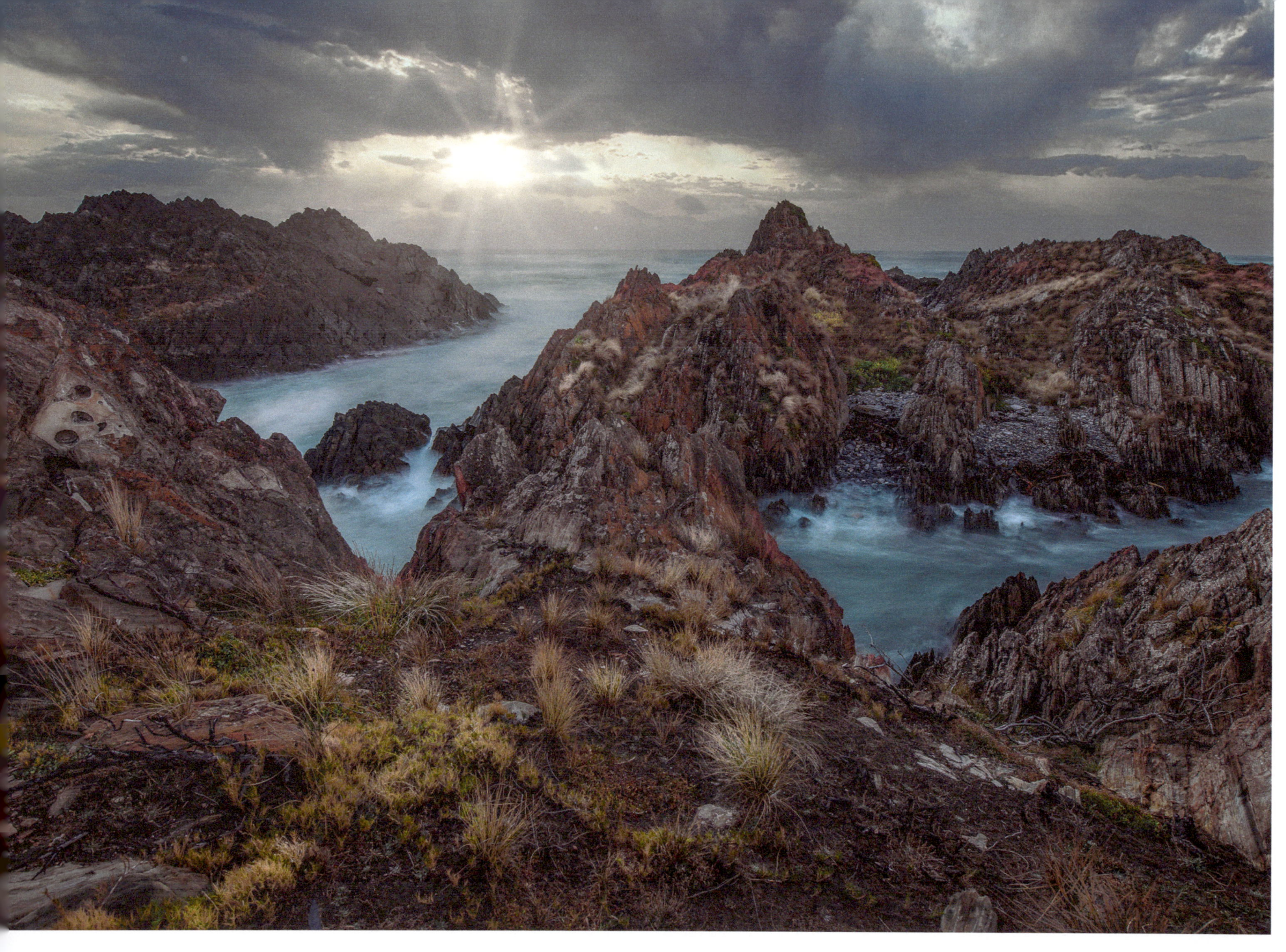

SARAH ANNE ROCKS

Breath is the ballast
Between the earth and the sky

Mind is the horse
On which we ride

As the spider spins the web
And the waves roll out to sea

May I cross the threshold
So that you can see me

Be the mind tamer
Soothe your hungry beast

So she becomes your mistress
Lying at your feet

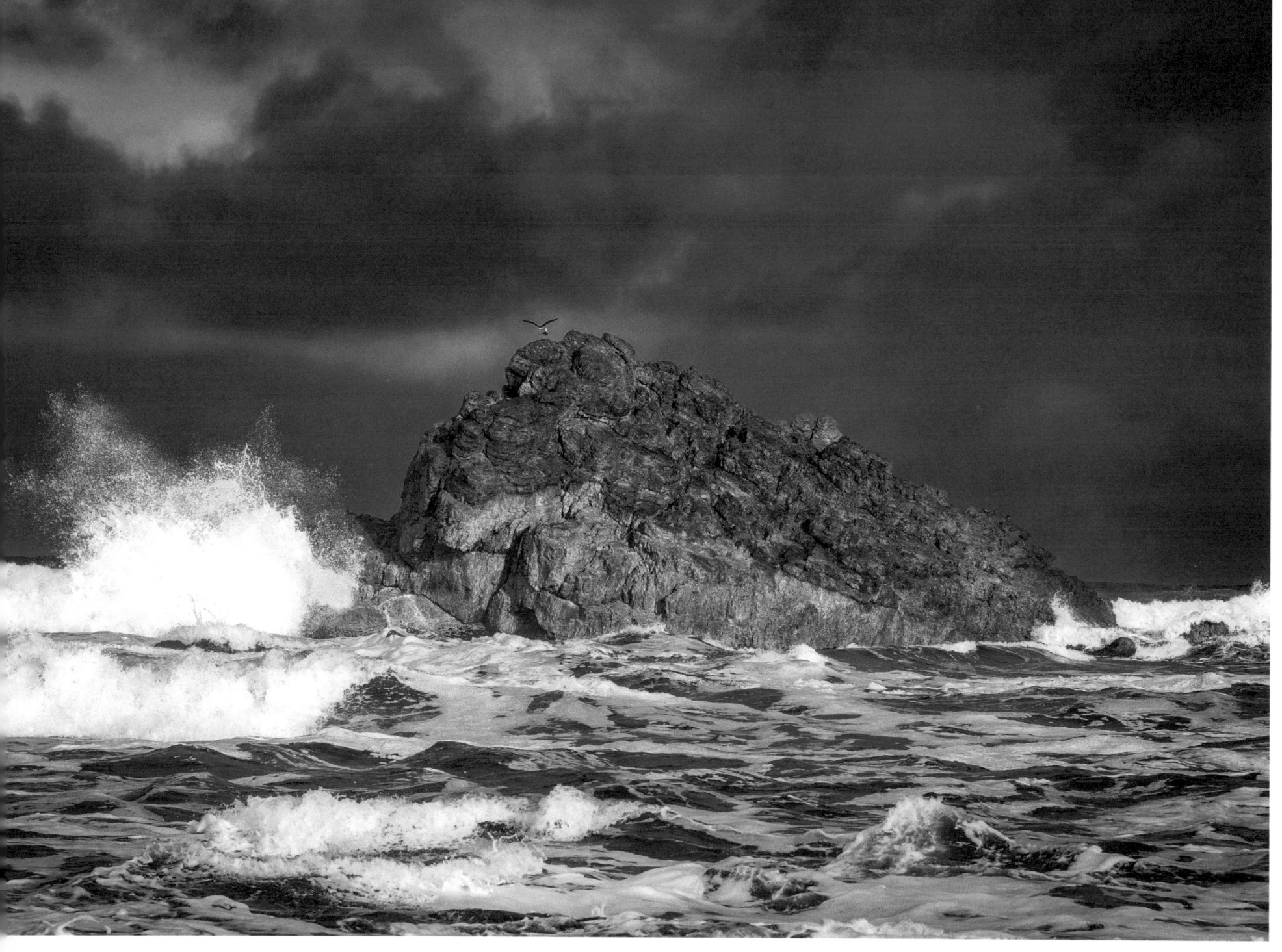
CHURCH ROCK, ARTHUR RIVER

I will carry you
I will cradle your heart

I will kiss you
And give you your fill
So you become whole

And all that dissolves
Was never meant
To have such a hold

The sorrows that hold me so
When will they disappear?
When will they let go?

When the mind dissolves
And the breath falls
Into the heart

When I fade away
And feel myself whole

When she holds my hand
Awakening my soul

When I feel your lips
And taste your kiss

When I feel my unfurling
And I know you are here

Come to me
For when we are together
I do not know fear

Come to my ocean
Calls the Beloved

But first you must sail on the river
Feel the winds whisper
My breath beneath your sail
My hand cupping your boat
Whilst setting you free

Until the river joins the ocean
And you are with me

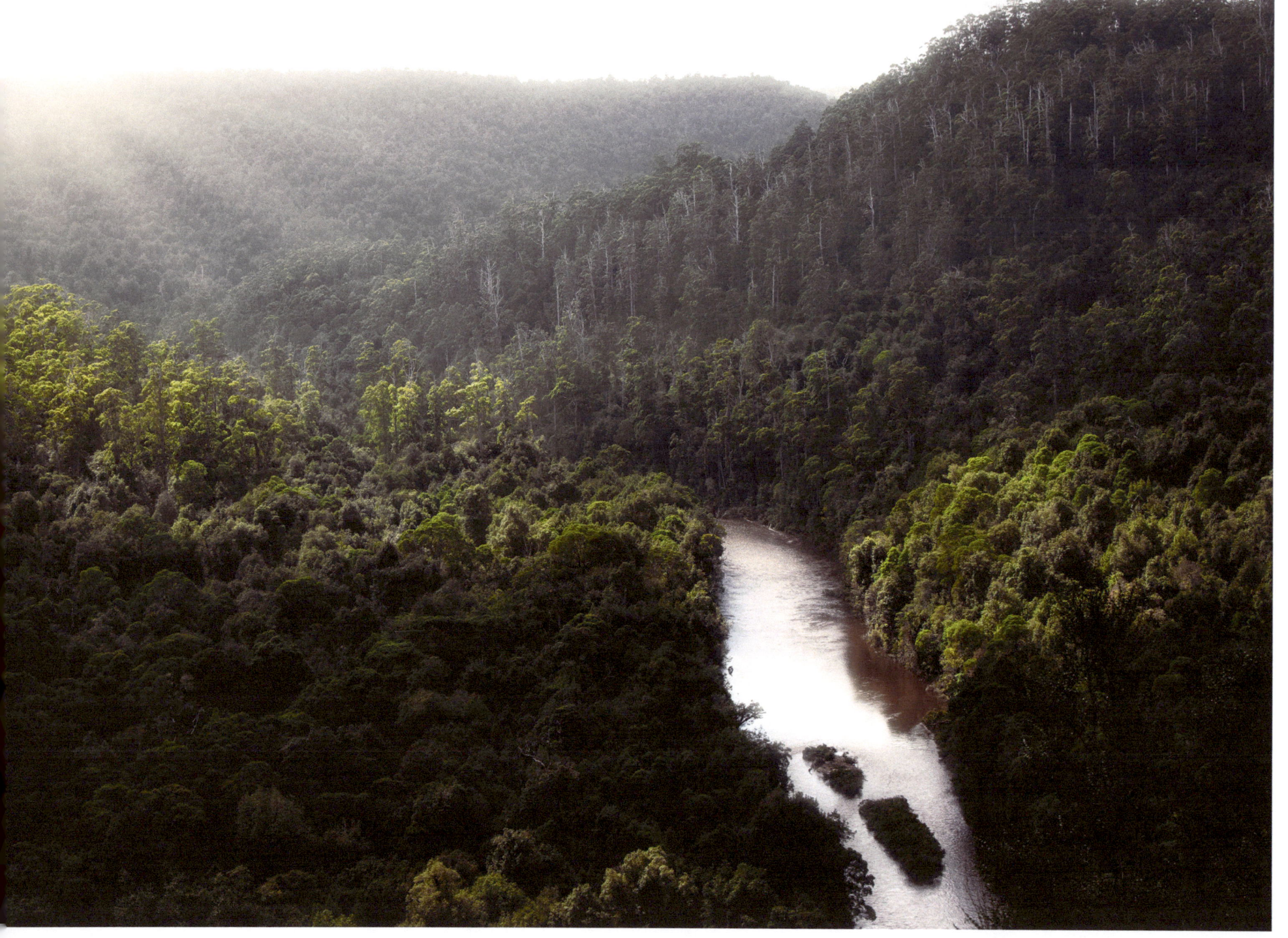

SUMAC LOOKOUT

3.

Fear and Loss

To the mind that is still, the whole universe surrenders.
– Lao Tzu

As I sit in your garden and ponder all you have made, I begin to truly wonder, how have we lost our way? How can I feel the love I am to receive? I get caught by my mind, the sorrow and fear. Trapped by the past, my body is so stuck with fear. Paralysed with panic and disconnection, I feel undone. I yearn to remember, to connect with us as One. Overwhelmed by the loss that I feel is impending.

How can my conditioning, my mind, fall away?
How can I relinquish all that I know?
How can I love your beautiful garden?
How can I hold my children so dear?
How can I cherish each and every moment?
How can I hold you, so very near?

When all that I fear, is the cataclysmic death, of all whom I love, all I hold so dear. Such a bind is the self, the paradox of One, within the duality, of self and your love.

How can I find myself, how can I dissolve my mind and its mess?

I know the only way through is to harness the mind and bow to the breath. Trust the love in my heart and forsake all the rest. But when the fear is so strong, eclipsing entirely, it is so very hard to know how to let go.

Who is dying? What is the real death?
Is death an illusion or a dissolving of self?

It is hard to remember the truth when I am lost in the trees.
Is all that I am fearing the death of false me?

Please show me the way, help me become clear. Light up the path, which takes me from fear. If all that is dying is my old self, please take my hand, lift me up high.

Show me the mountains, show me the sky
Show me your love, your omnipresence, your breath
Open my heart, water my seed
Show me the flower inherent in me

Please take my hand, show me how to be
Let me fall at your feet, let me be free
Help me come back to the essence within
So I may finally know the truth within me
Let me return, let me love you
So I can help others
Who are yearning for you, too.

If all that I know is to hold on tight, how can I learn to truly let go?

My fist clenched tense from all that I fear, I shrivel, not knowing you are near. Yet, in my moments of lucidity, when I feel you, I realise all was an illusion, I was only a moment from 'here'.

What is here but the moment of Now? When the vibration around me, so strong and clear, announces your arrival, it illuminates the sphere. With your luminescence, my heart enlivens, as though all before was only flesh, caught in the mire of earthly design.

Life is only an illusion, so I am told. Hard to comprehend in this world of fear and sorrow. Love intertwines, yet all falls through my fingers. Here is nothing we can permanently hold.

I am but a vessel for you to fill. Pour your wine into me, my love. Touch me with your lips, let me be no longer bereft. Move through my emptiness. When I feel your presence, all is eclipsed.

Let me be the chalice to hold your sacred wine. Turn my flesh to dust and let my old self die. Touch me for a lifetime, take my hand, drink from me, so I can finally understand. All that I yearn for, all that is real, is in your heart, the love I feel.

May I gaze upon your face and bow to you, Beloved. Let me into your sacred space. Drink, come to me now. Unclench my hand, for all the sorrow to fall, the fear to dissolve, as love blossoms for all.

Open your palm to me. Let me kiss your hand, for therein lies the seed, no longer made of sand, but a beautiful flower, a chrysalis of love, waiting for me.

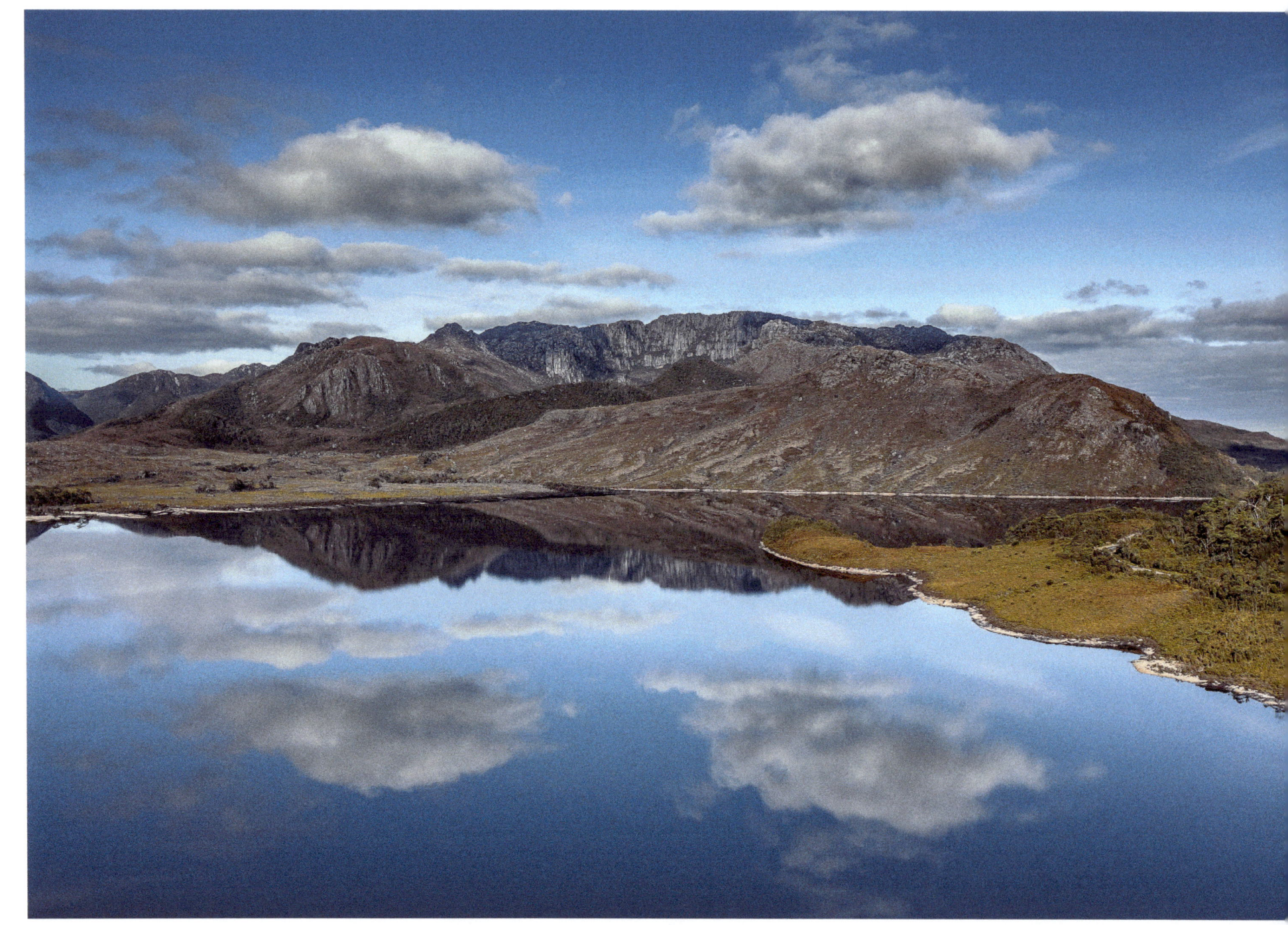
LAKE PLIMSOLL

4.

Longing and Devotion

Light will come to thee from longing.
— Sufi poet from Sindh

Extract from Irina Tweedie, *The Chasm of Fire: A Woman's Experience of Liberation*

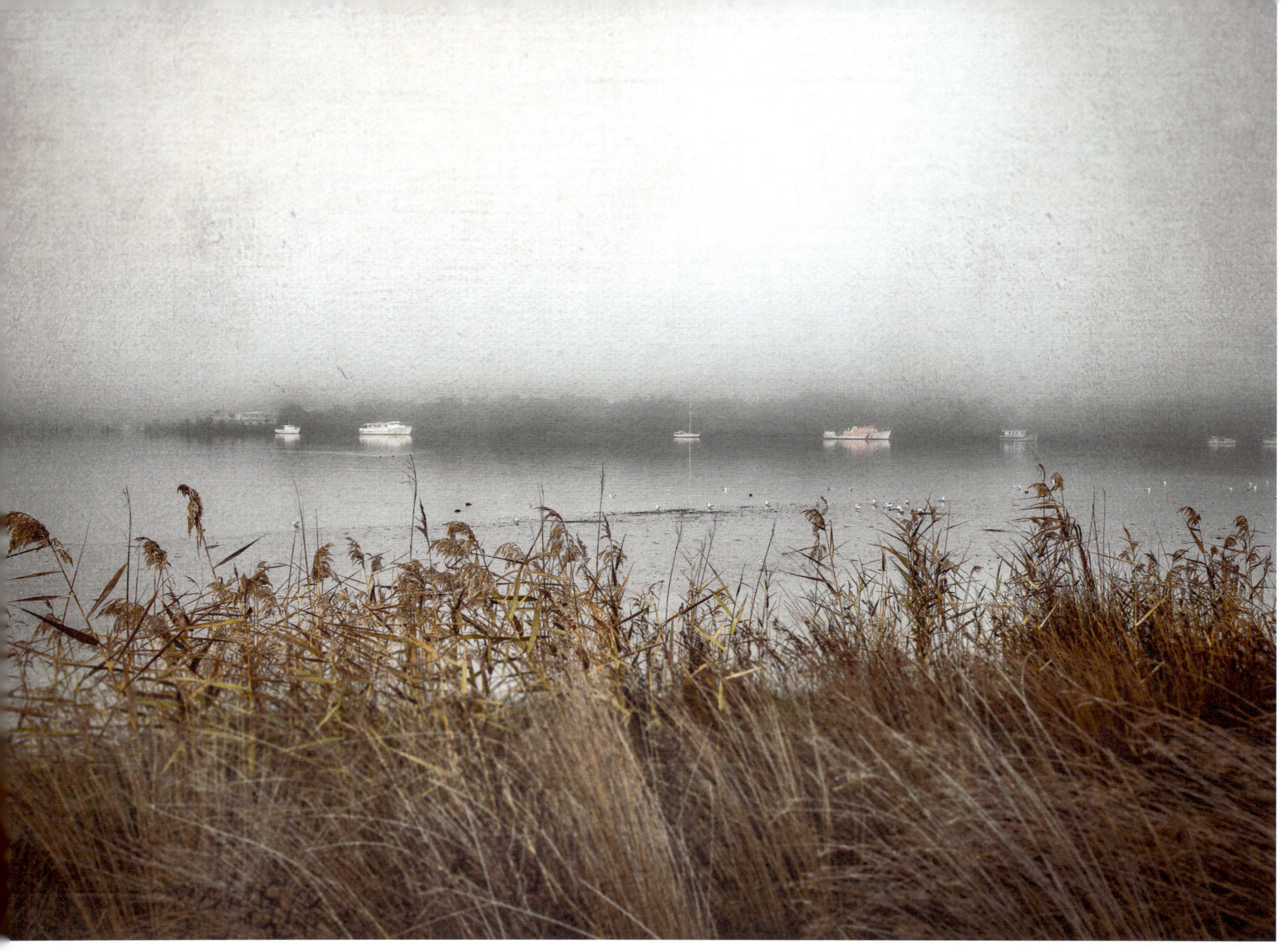

TAMAR RIVER, LAUNCESTON

We Seek Outside For What Is Within

Is this a gift from the Beloved?

To remind me
Of what's true?

This sweetness of love
This liquid longing
This insatiable hunger

This yearning for you

May I breathe in your grace

As I look through the window
And feel your gaze

Upon my face

May our hearts bleed
Not of loss

But of the love

Which speaks
Between you and me

Without pain
We become who we truly are

Not a reflection of self
But a mirror so clear
To see you again

I cannot contain her
For she is not to be mine

Rather

She slips through my fingers
Like nectar and wine

Beloved
I am just here

Beloved
Please see me

Beloved
I am at your door
Yearning to be free

Oh, Beloved
All is eclipsed
When I feel you, with me

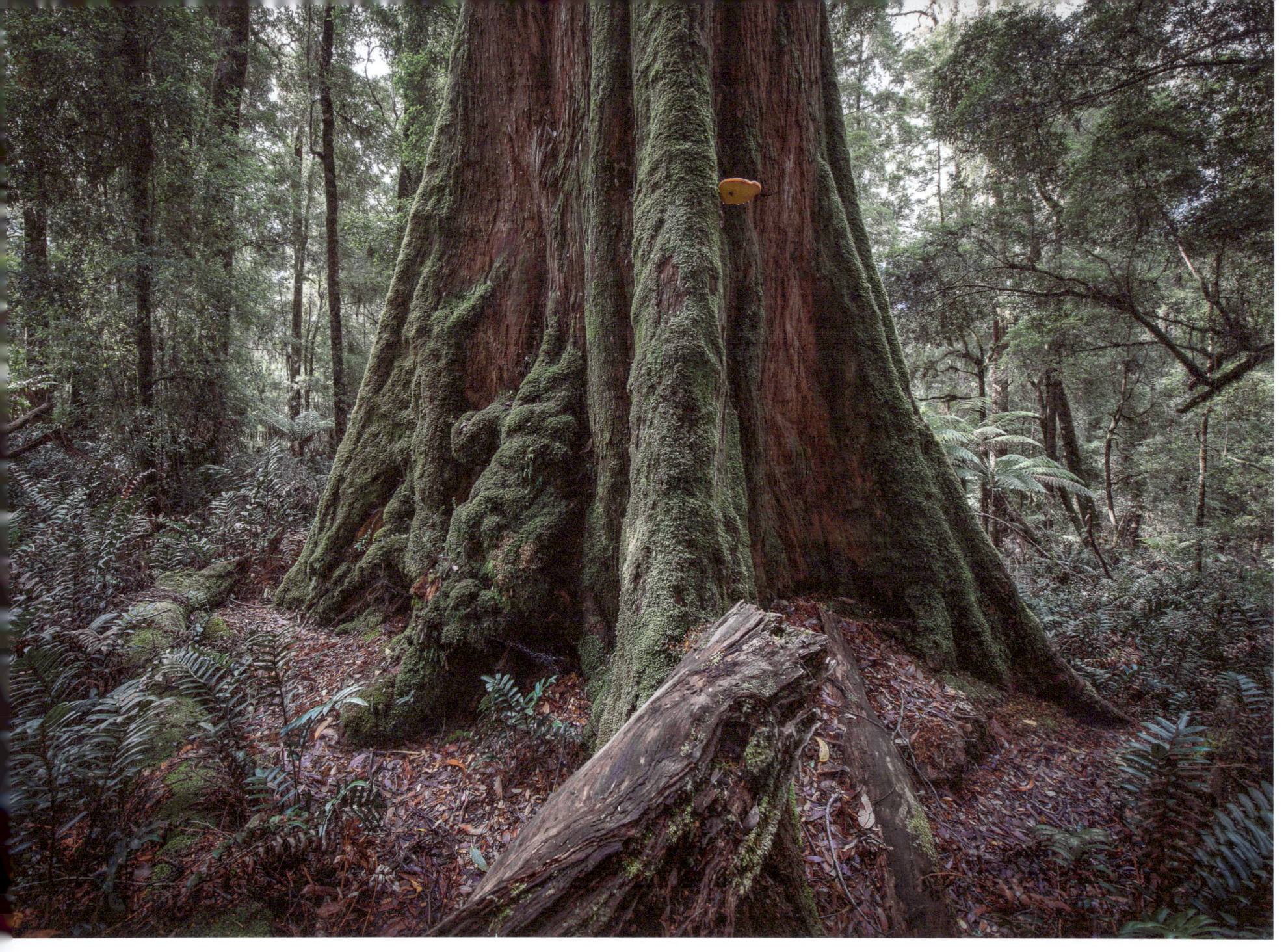

SAVAGE RIVER NATIONAL PARK

The river in our heart
Flows through time, carries our spark
Breathe her in, dissolve all sorrows
Allow the ripples to flow, into you

Breathe in deep, let your heart stand still
Just for a moment
Feel your spark, drop into the ripple
Sink deep below

Caught in the undercurrent
As I feel the undertow, deep into the pools
Far below
And there I find you
Deep below, always here
Once again, life will show

That love is a waterfall, enveloping all around
You are the vibration, within the particle of sound
You are the vibration, that lives in my name

I am the vibration, carried in the flame
Held in the well, found deep below
Carrying all bliss
As all that is formed, not burdened or hollow
Yet clear and true

As slowly, each lifetime
I find my way, back to you

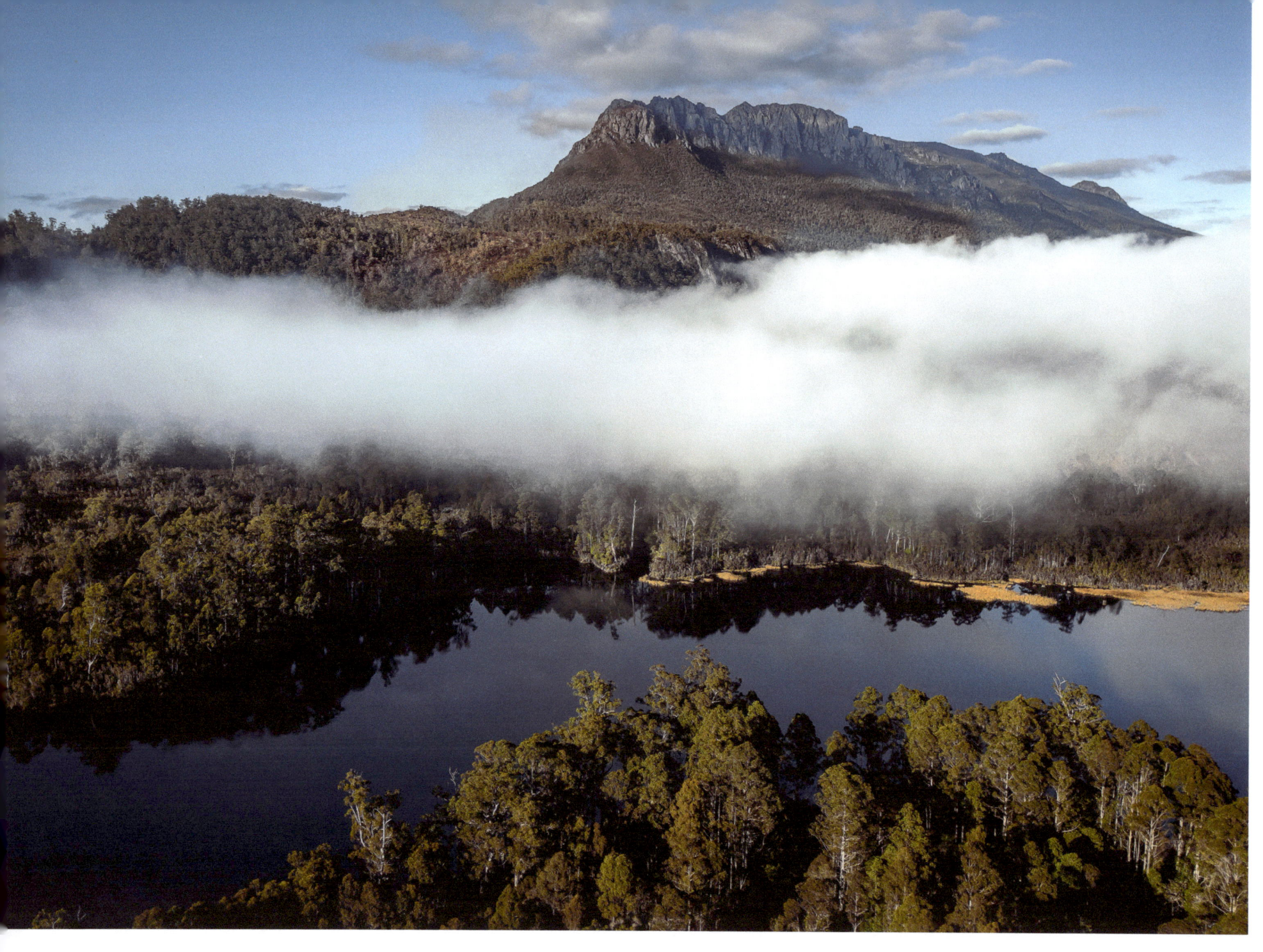

MOUNT MURCHISON, TULLAH

Liberated beings
Speak of no attachment

All must let go
To break free

All must let go
To finally see

My hand curls around the key
Unlocks the door
To your heart

Oh, Beloved
Let me
Be free

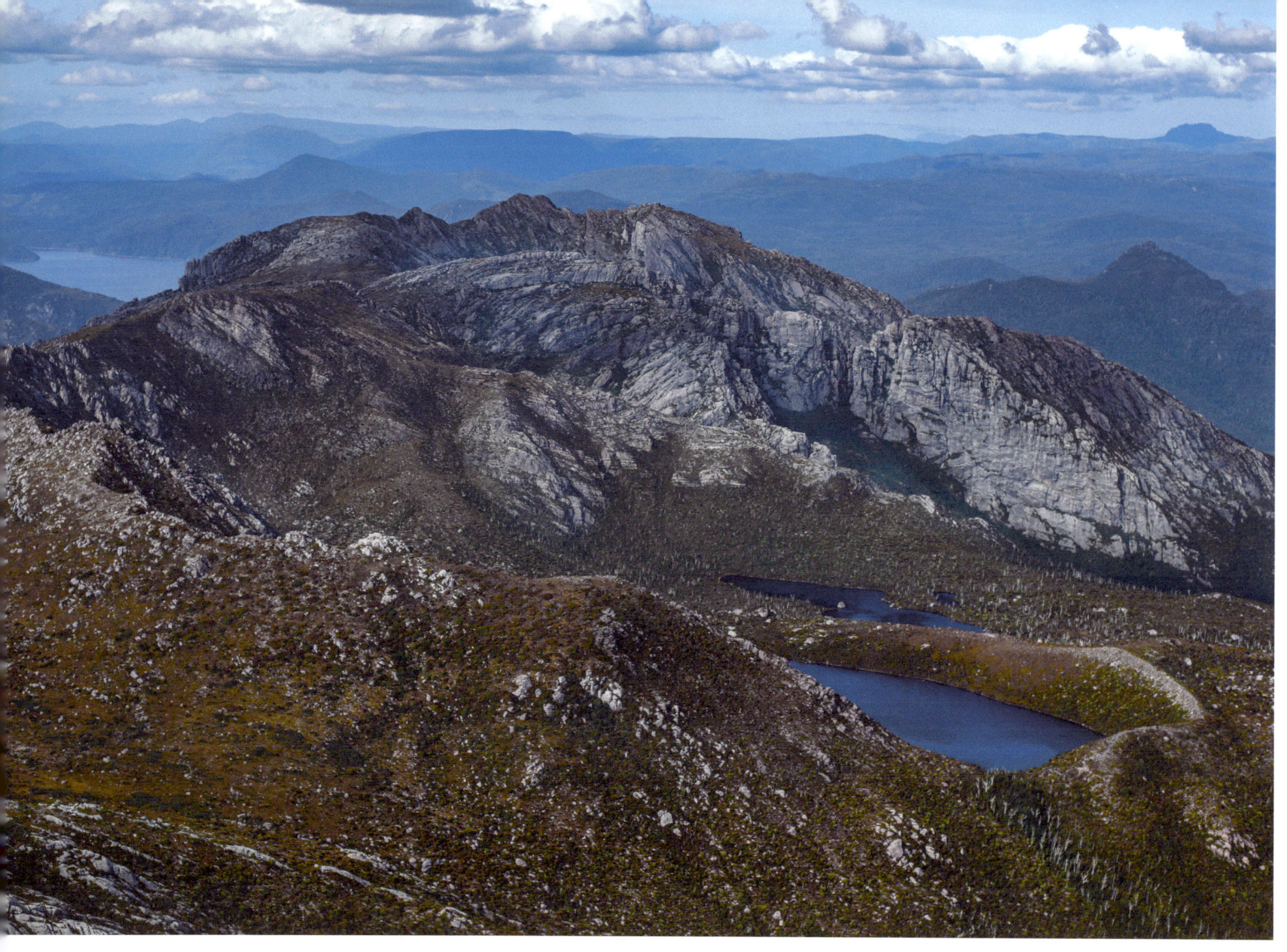

NORTH-CENTRAL TASMANIA

Beloved

To feel you again
When I am so parched and dry
A blind soul in the desert
No flowers, no shrine

To feel for a moment
Your touch
Your breath
Your heartbeat

To remember my purpose
Wake from my sleep
To realise I was, but a dream

Let your love flow through me
Soft and gentle
Bowing within, feeling your grace
All that I was
A momentary state

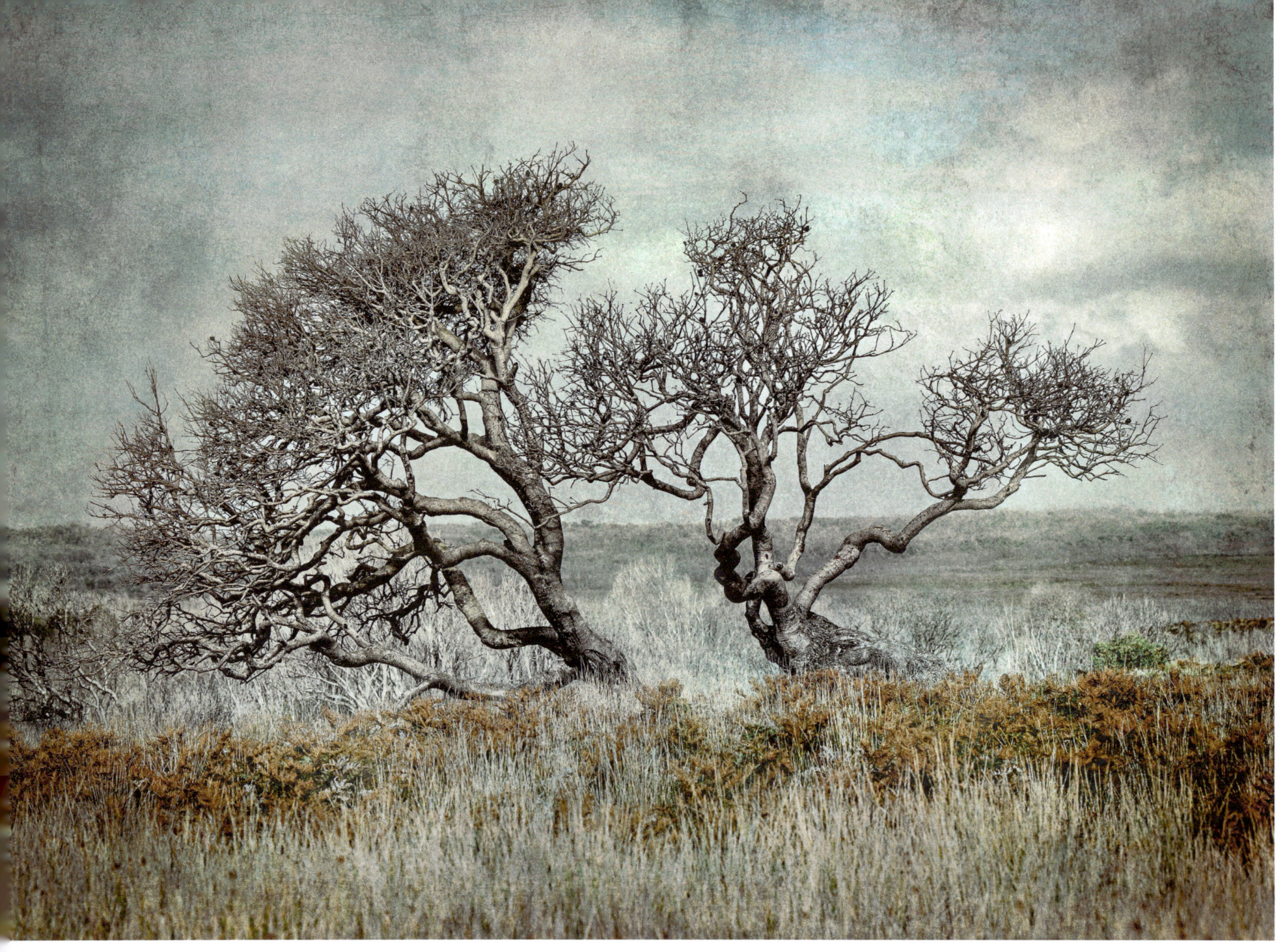

NELSON BAY

May I walk through the Valley of the Shadow of Death
Unencumbered
Not broken
But free

May I walk through the Valley of the Shadow of Death
Where the Beloved holds my hand
Whilst liberating me

May I walk through the Valley of the Shadow of Death
The luminescence of the heart
Marking my path

May I walk through the Valley of the Shadow of Death
Until I find the place
Where we exist
Outside time and space

May I walk through the Valley of the Shadow of Death
To find my true rest
Held in the palm of your hand

Held in your heart
Not just of God or Gaia
But the beauty within
Which crowns us all

The Divinity of our heart
May we heed the call

Be with me now
So I may burn inside

Open me up
Break me in two

Let me in
Let me love
You

If the path to you
Is fraught with pain

Let me take my first step
So I may see you, again

Who will I be
When I am
Carried out to sea?

Just a beacon of light
So you can follow me

The heart does not know its desolation
Until the Beloved's caress

Cupped by Divinity
It blooms
Like an oasis

Teeming with fragrance
It finally knows
It is home

May I be a light for others to see
May I feel you with me

May I be a piercing light
To transcend the dark

May I be a light of transformation
May my love pour into you

Break open the shell
That covers your heart

No longer a seed thirsty or dry
But a flower held in my hand

Feel my heartbeat synchronise with yours
Feel me knock
As I open your door

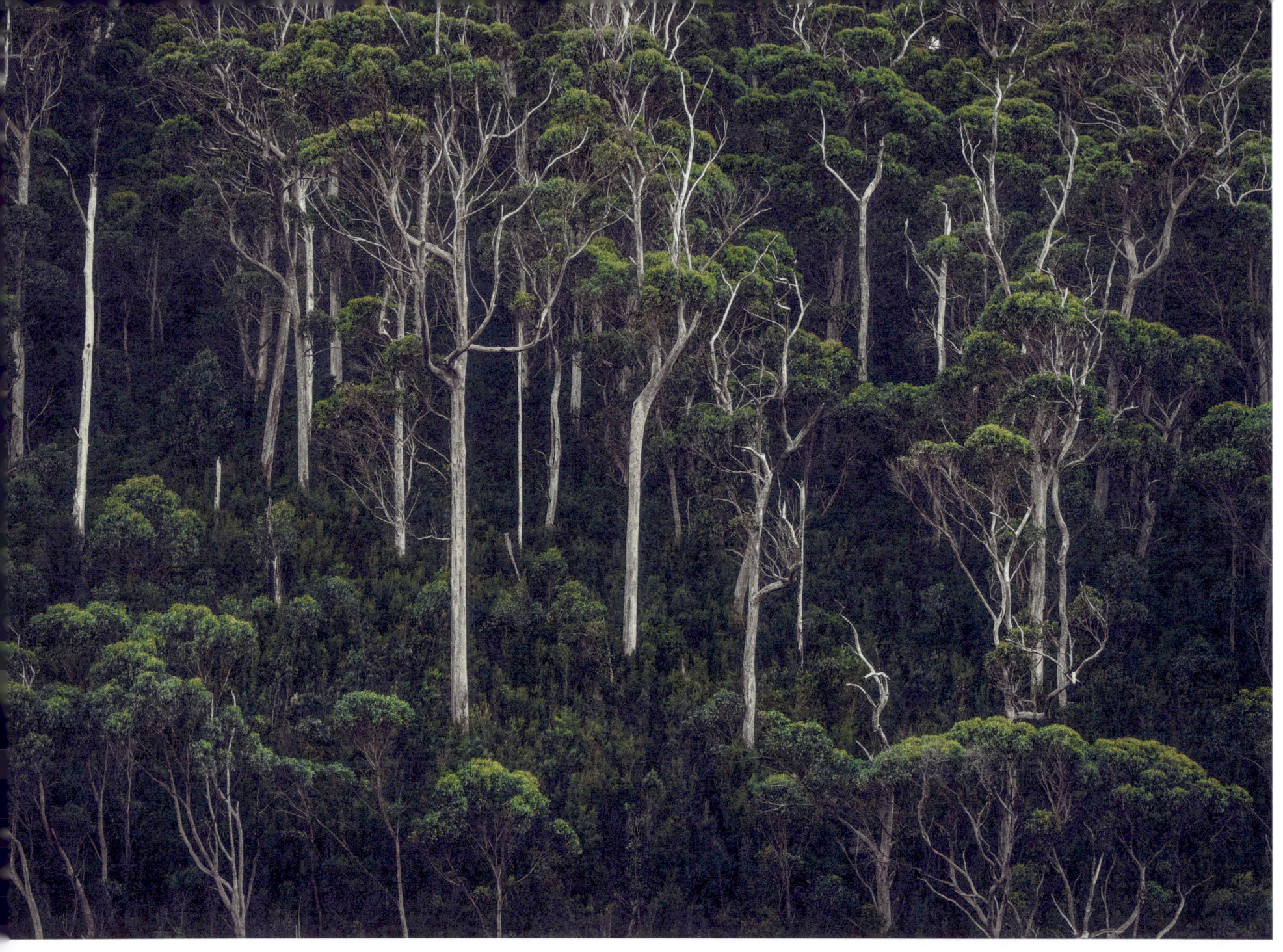
CORINNA TARKINE/takayna

Beloved
As I float out to sea
I can feel you call me

Beloved
Hold my hand, so I may feel your warmth
And come to understand

Beloved
Kiss my lips, so I may taste your nectar
And feel your bliss

Beloved
Let me drink your wine, feel my heart unfold
As I dissolve into Divine

Beloved
May I feel your breath, inhale
And know my own death

Beloved
Pray, come to me

Pass the cup, let me drink
Hold me close, feel me sink
Into you

Inextricably linked, not of sorrow
But of love
Before time became true

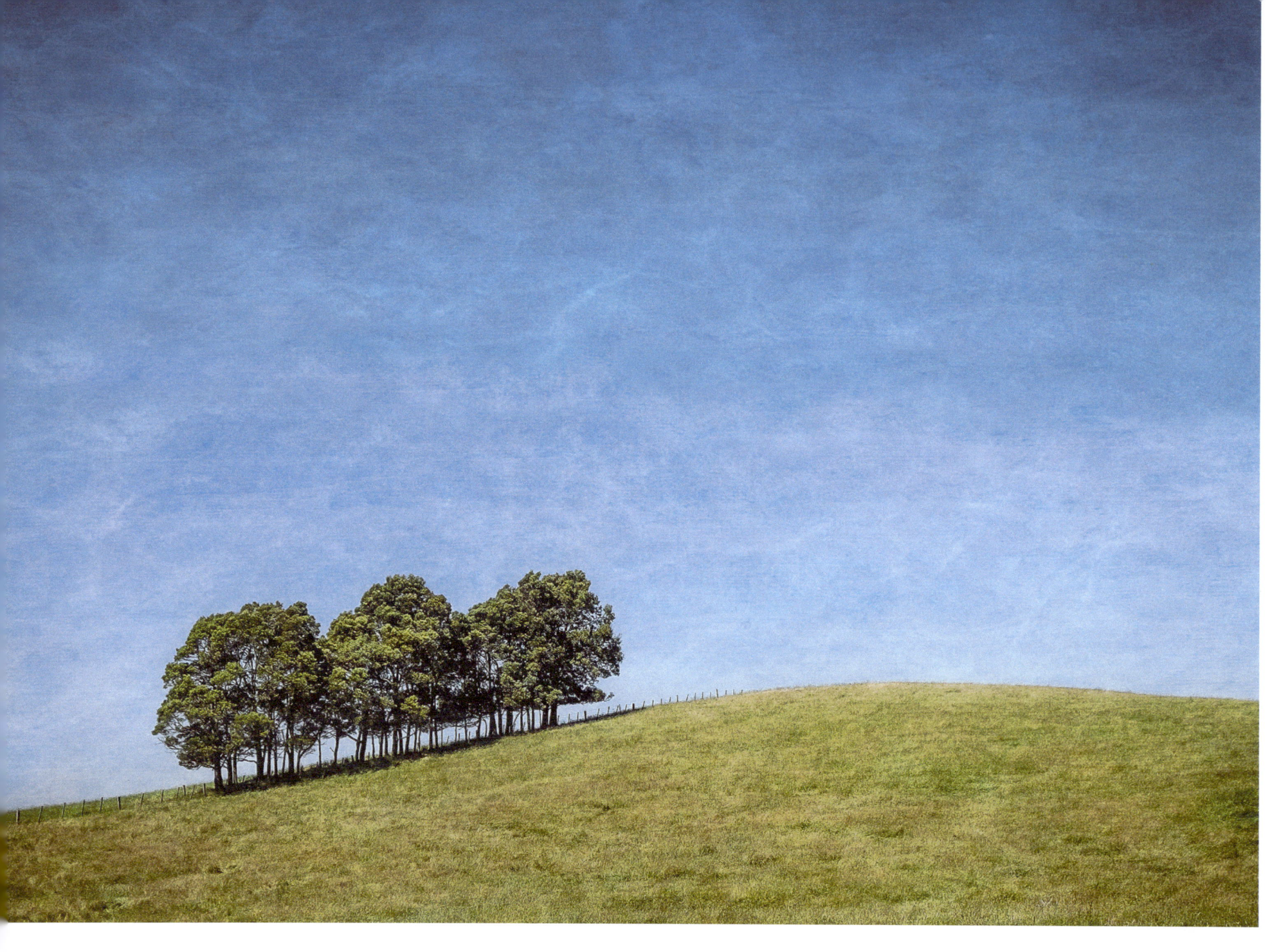

FARMLAND, LEBRINA

Our inner cosmos
Is made of flowers and beautiful things

Sun streams in, illuminating our sphere
This sacred energy
Our soul intelligence
Defines us deep within

I was weary and worn
Longing for love
But now I see
That which I had forgotten
Blossoms inside me

All my yearnings
Were in vain
For you were always here
Fanning my flame

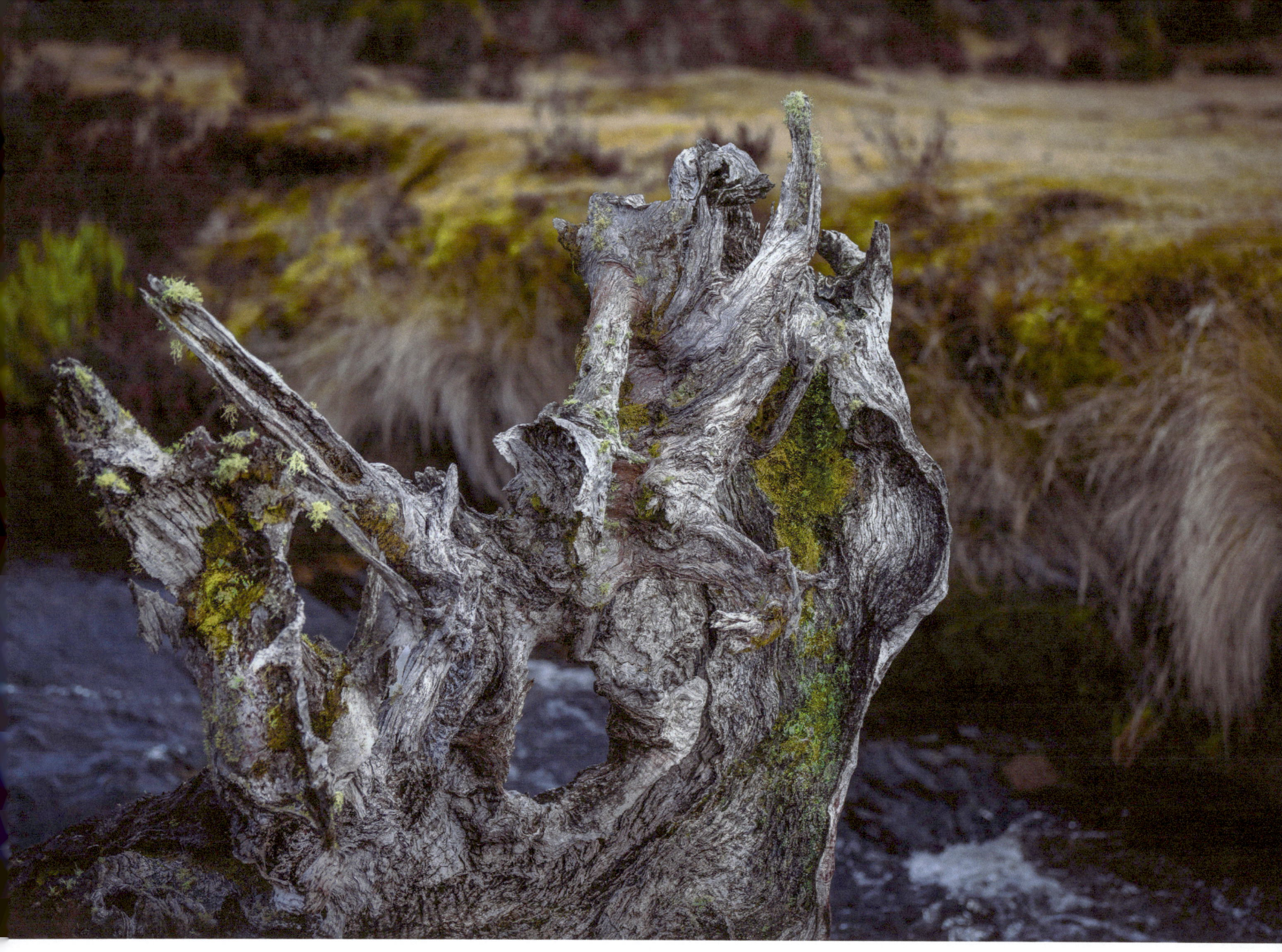

CENTRAL PLATEAU

5.

The Essence

*Make everything in you an ear, each atom of your being, and you will hear at every moment
what the Source is whispering to you, just to you and for you, without any need for my words or anyone else's.*
 – Rumi

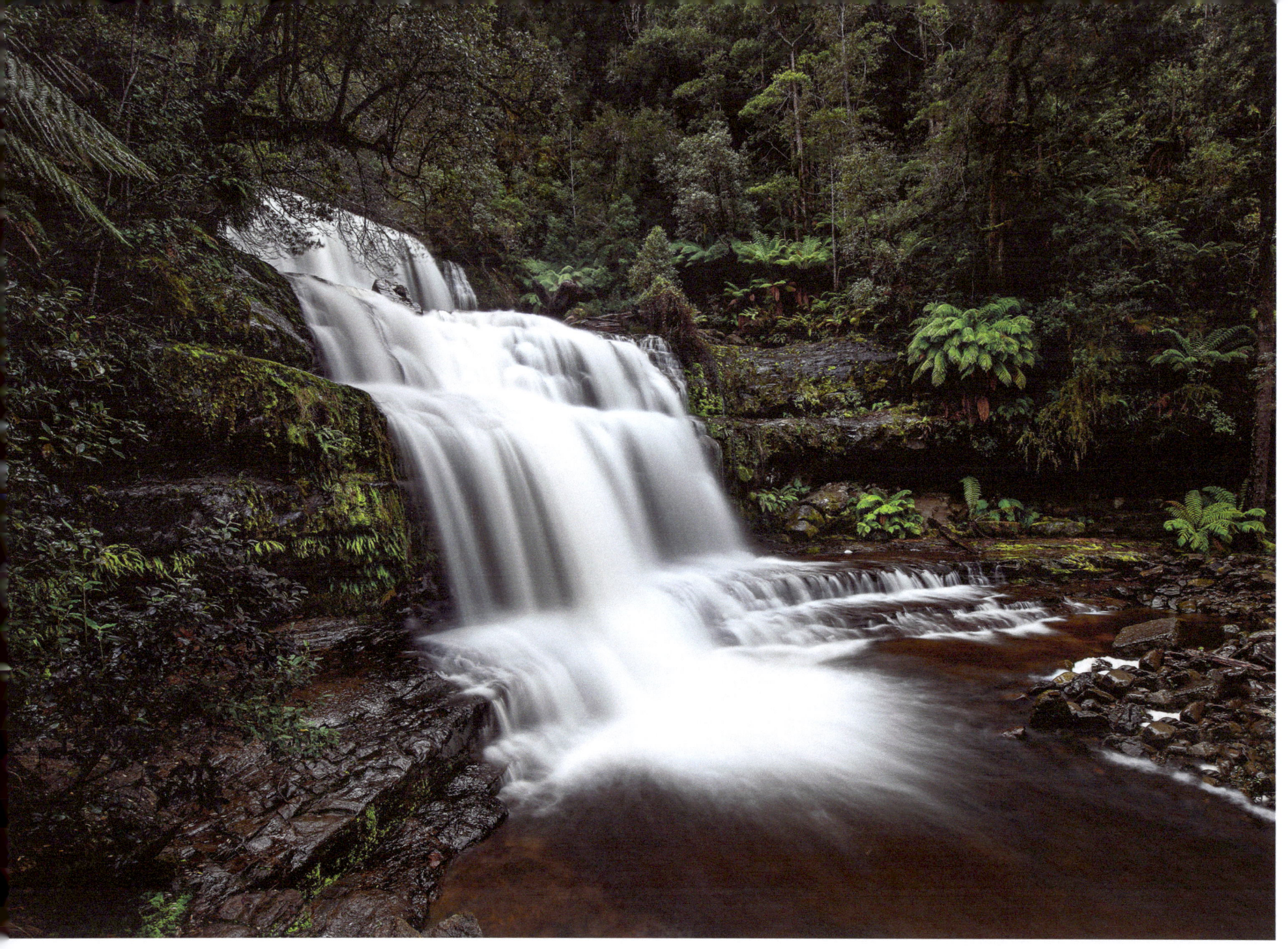

LIFFEY FALLS

Your hearts's inheritance is within the sacred seed

Your seed needs to burn
To unfold

Consciousness is carried in the heart

My heart led me through her garden
Oh what a joy

In coming to Be!

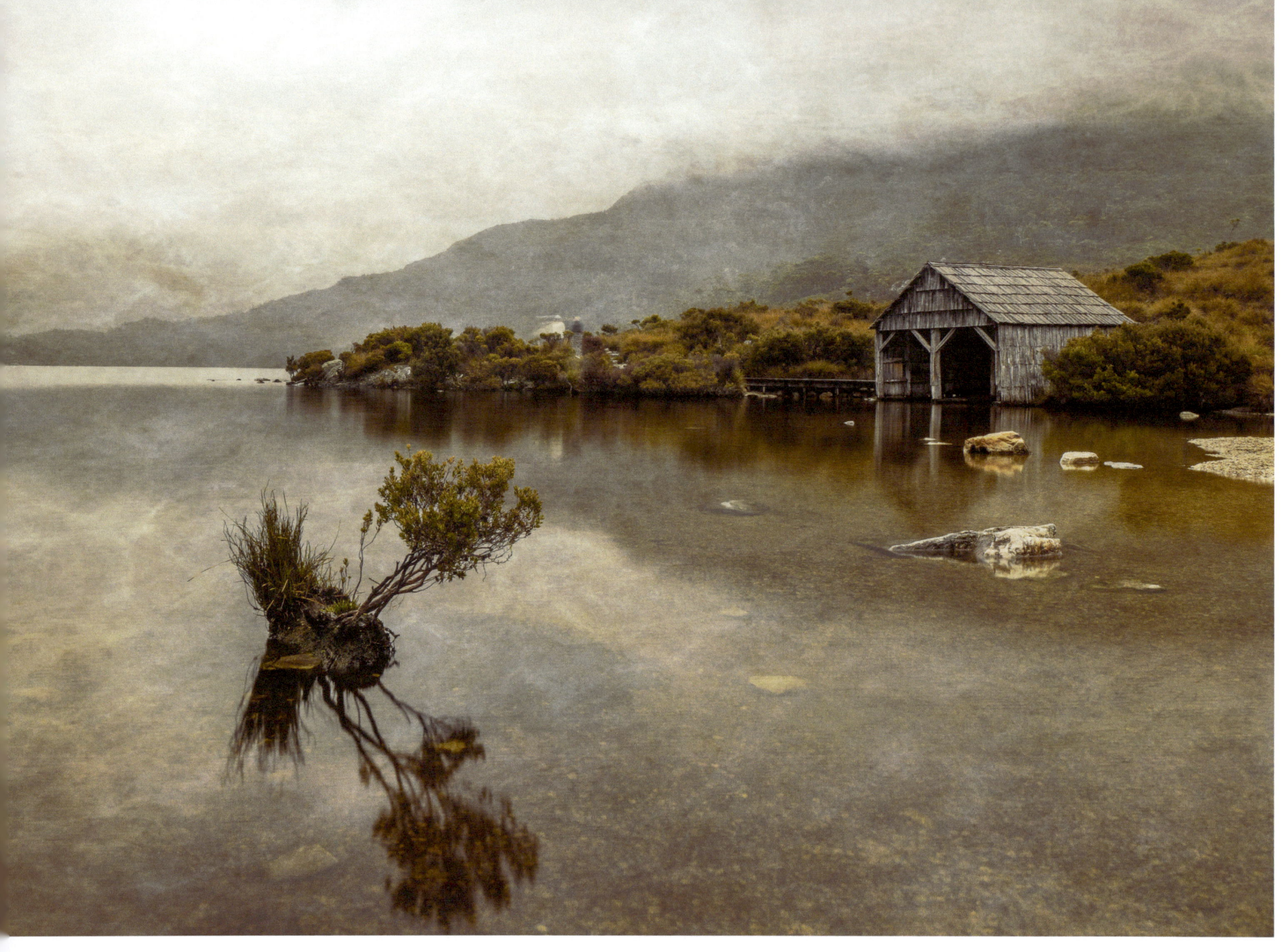

CRADLE MOUNTAIN NATIONAL PARK

My heart doesn't settle
In pools of sadness
As it used to

Since I found
The love that ripples
Underground

For what I do not know
With the heart
Is empty knowledge

Just a bare twig on a vine
Unable to bear fruit
Or make wine

There are universes within the heart
Beyond our rubies and gold

The universes within
Are not for us to hold
There are sacred realms beyond
Beckoning to us all

The universe within
Where the Beloved calls
Inviting us to dance
When we finally fall

Go where the Beloved is
Resplendent
Luminous
Awaiting us all

Our universe within
Is lit by a trillion stars
Take my hand
Come with me
I will show you
Your inner door

Be still
Drink from within
And feel your heart
Eclipse us all

Beloved

From fear to love
Thought to awareness
Breath to the river of God

At the merging of the waters
I finally see you

As I drink from the heart
And feel deep inside
All that I am
Is sacred and alive

Turn the key
Open the door
And you will see

May I drink her wine
So that all I may be

Is held in the heart
Of Divinity

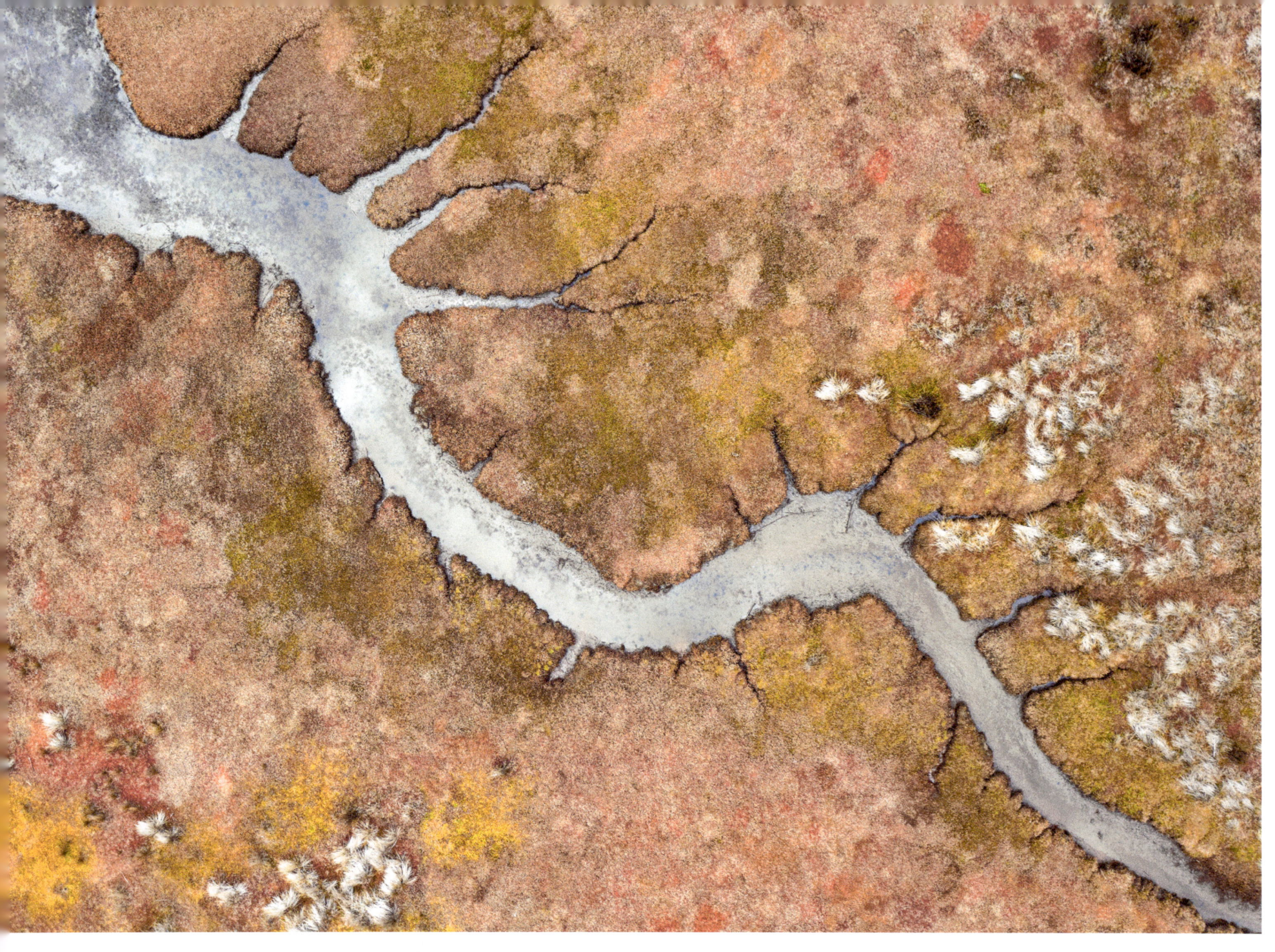

DRONE IMAGE, WETLANDS, CYGNET

She pulls me in
Holds me close
I disappear
Into the flow

All that I am
All that I know
Is carried within
Me and you

Just on the surface
Yet found deep below

I will not forsake her touch
For it gives my heart its beat

Hold me through the shadow
So I may come to know your light

I will not forsake the cradle
That holds me in my sleep

Burn me with your touch
So my heart may feel your beat

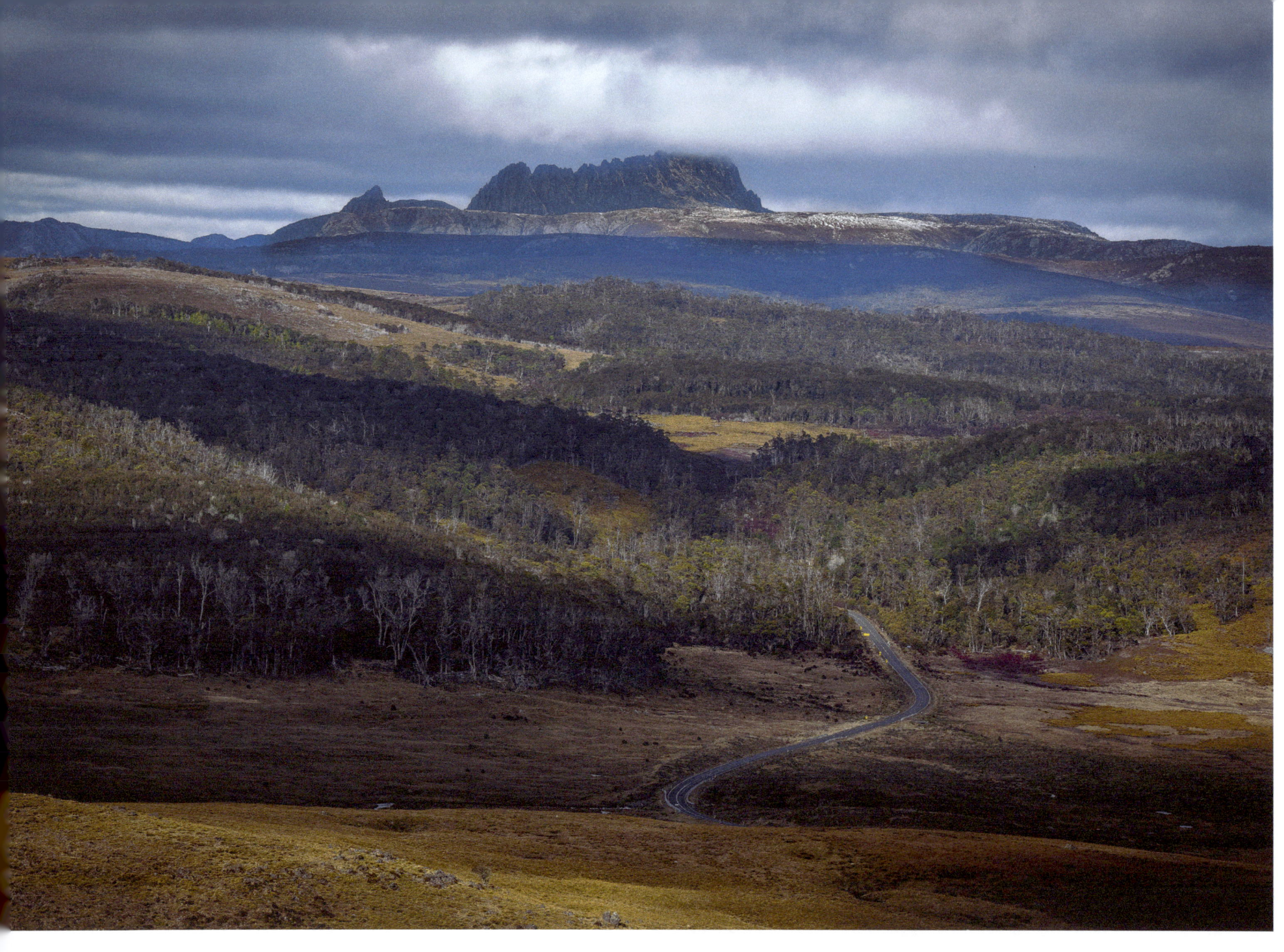

CRADLE MOUNTAIN

Am I just matter?
A buzzing collection of molecules?

Or perhaps a beacon of light?
A soul on a journey?
A spirit in flight?

How can we recognise the Divine
When we don't know ourselves?

How can we recognise ourselves
When we don't know the Divine?

How will I come to know her
If all I see is me?

How will I come to know her
If I can't rouse myself from sleep?

How will I come to know her
How will I dive so deep

If all I am is clouded by shadow
And my heart lies inert beneath?

I am here
I know no fear

Dissolve your mind away
As she comes to stay

And you feel her presence
In every breath

I feel awareness growing
With every step

Be with me, she calls

Let me hold your hand
Feel my heart
Inhale the scent

For I carry your flower
No longer a seed
In the palm of my hand

For you are truly
Now Free

If we can't access peace through stillness
Then it was never really gold

It was only dust
Not for us to hold

Let me Awaken
Let me float out to sea

Please take my hand
In coming to be

All falls away
I can finally feel
My heart seed

For I am here
Now
In coming to Be

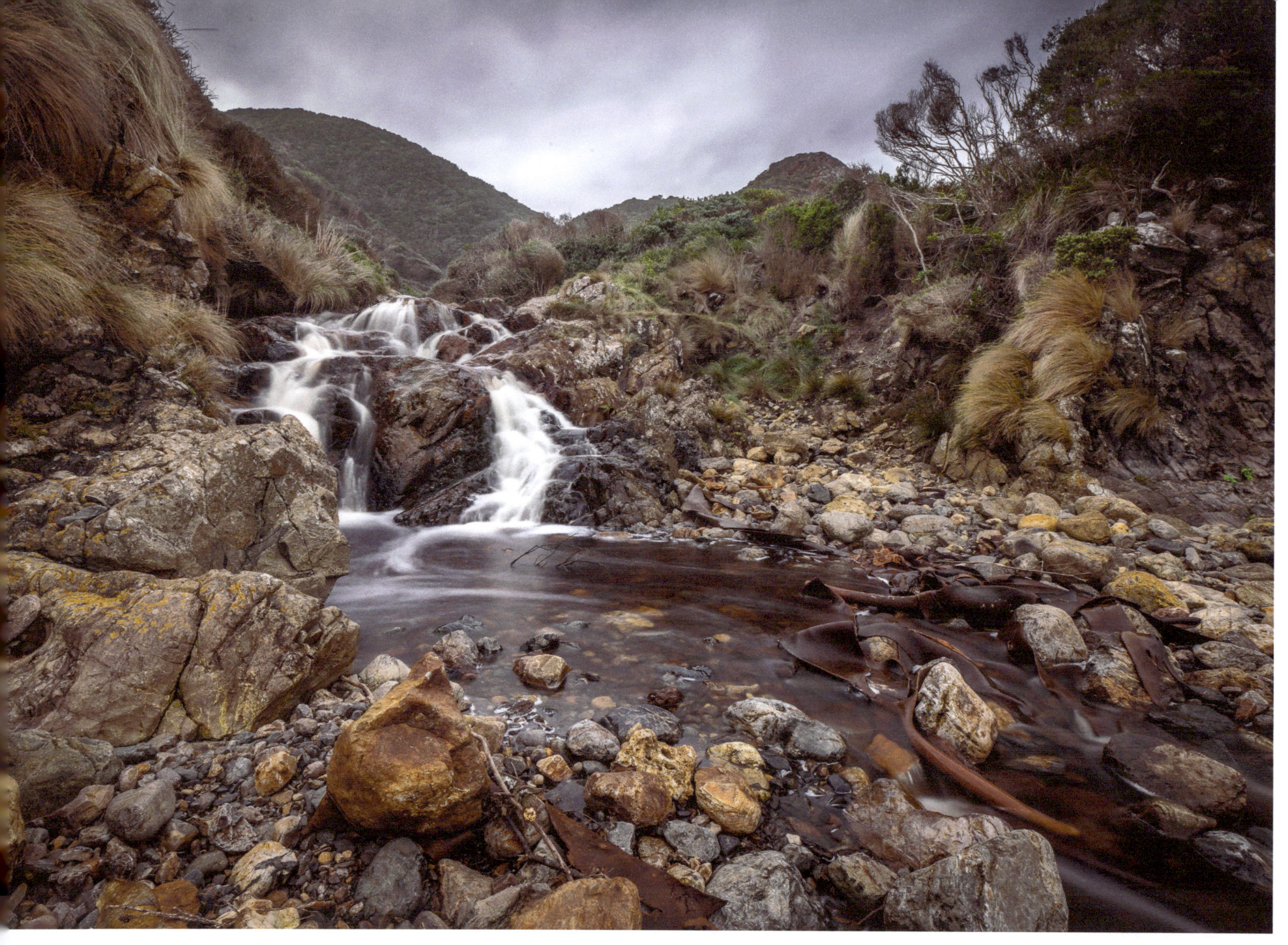

TRIAL HARBOUR

When you let go of life
It holds you

A chrysalis
A butterfly

All that I am

A metamorphosis
In coming to be

To be held by the heart
Is to know your truth

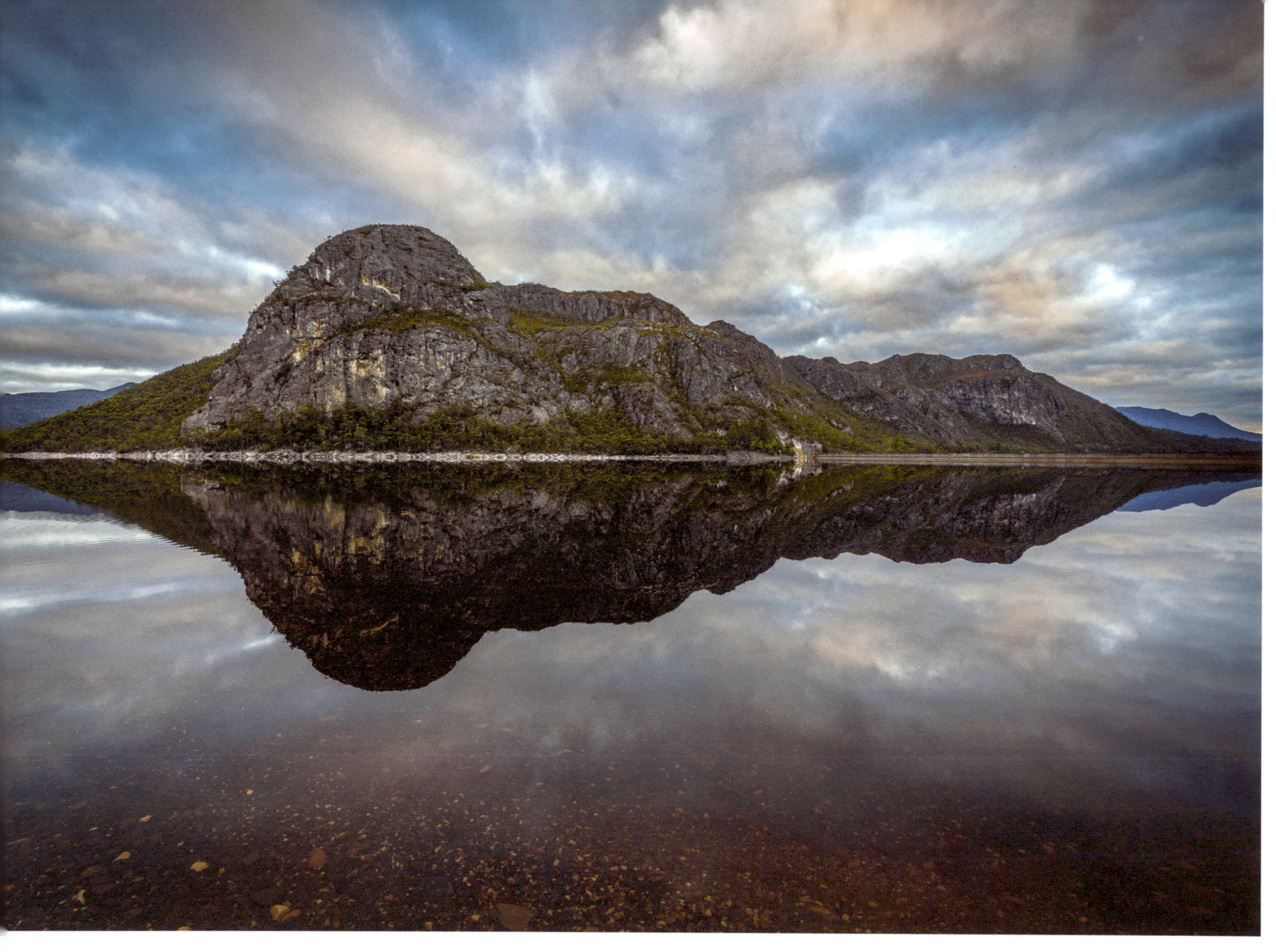

MACINTOSH DAM, TULLAH

A flower blossoms
On the surface
Of a still pool

All is alive
Resplendent

As I come
Back to you

The heart has to be
Strong in compassion
To truly break free

Compassion is the light
Particles of love
Luminescent and ripe

As they rain down
Falling on our skin
Another star is born
Within the flow
Of you and me

Please let me gaze into your heart
Please let me see your soul

For when I see you
And when you see me

We
Are all I know

Please let me gaze
Within the space between
Where your love flows
And I come to be seen

Please let me gaze
Let me understand
All that I am, only a flower

All that I am
Now a spark of Divinity
Gently cupped in your hand

When we realise
We are an infinitesimal spark
Just waiting to catch
To blossom, to grow

All is revealed
Within a galaxy of stars
Neither above or below
But carried inside us
Waiting to show

No finer truth
Can be told through time

Our heart is a place
For our soul to rest

Our heart is the realm
Of pure love and bliss

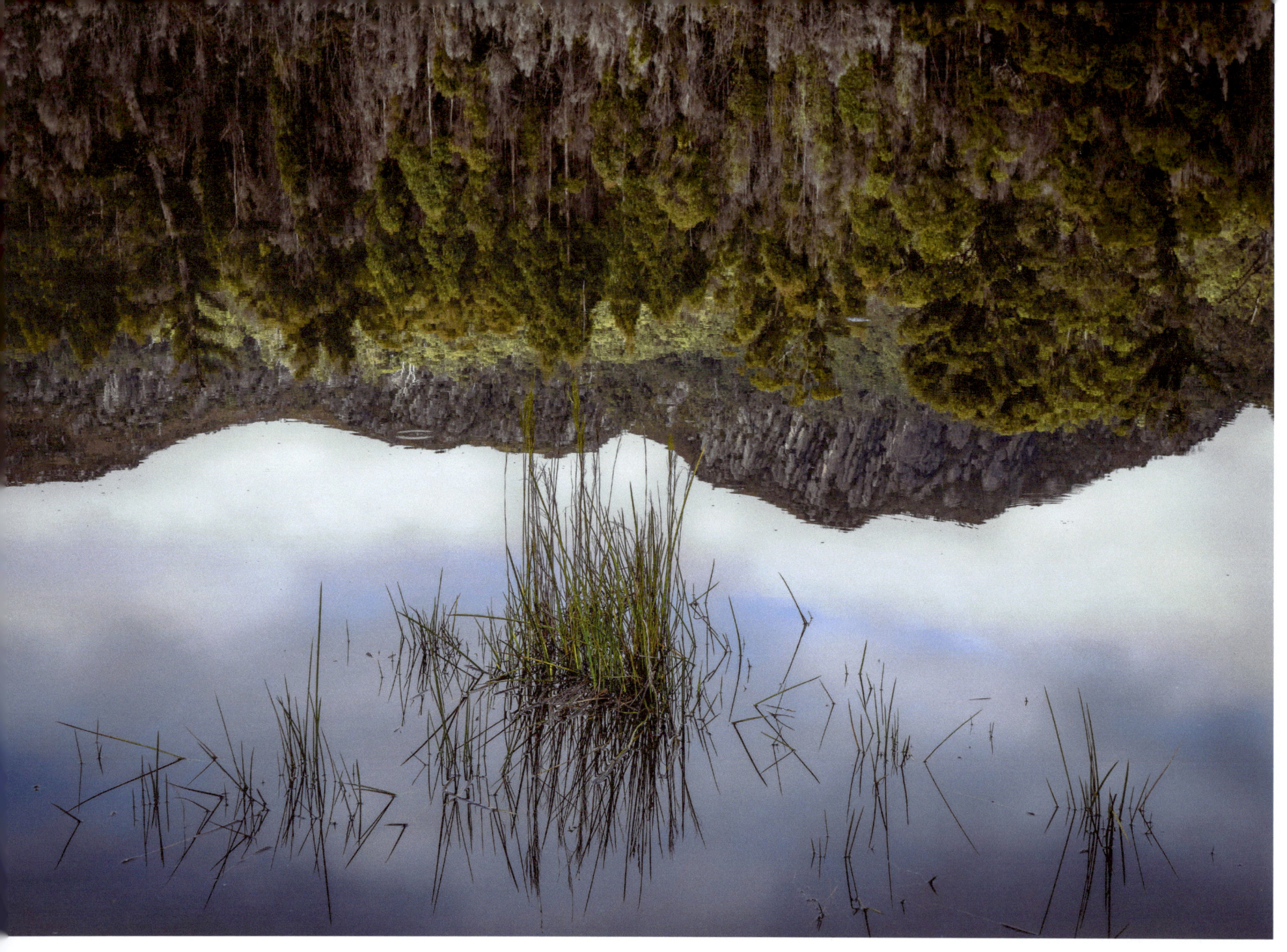

LAKE ROSEBERY, TULLAH

Am I the rock or the water?
Do I cultivate the stillness
Or caress the rock
With flow?

I am neither, yet both

For when I come to understand
The nature of mind
I realise
I am the flow and the stillness

I am the sweat on your brow
The ticking through time
I am beyond the earth and the sky

I am the beat of your heart
A magnetic flow
I am the seed in the soil
Waiting to grow

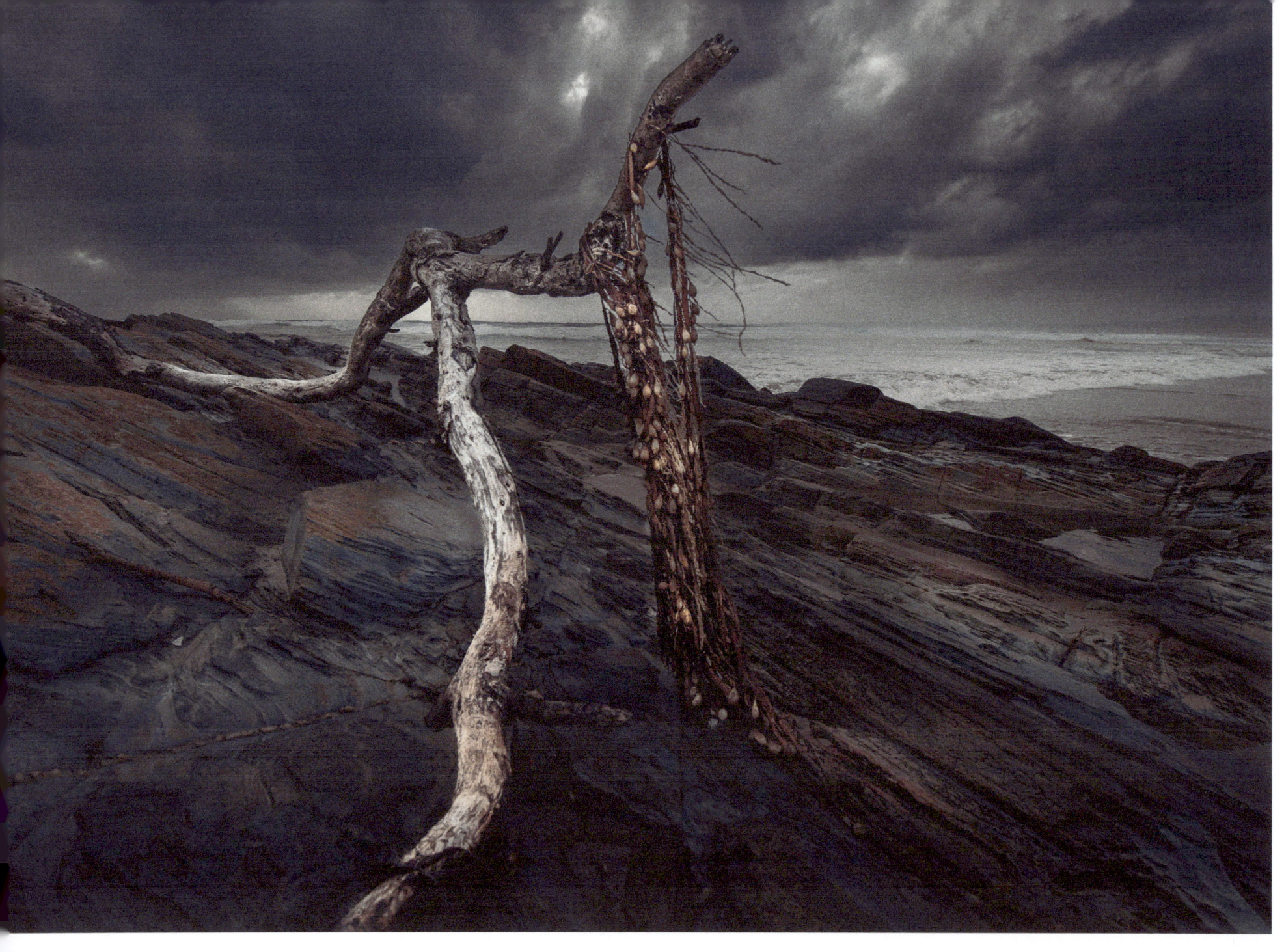

COUTA ROCKS

Oh, Beloved

We finally kiss

We dissolve
Slip away
Into your caress

Ready and waiting
To fall into our bliss

Let me behold
Your lotus flower
In a myriad of ways

Scented and sweet
As I fall at your feet

Your hand reaching out
To enfold mine
As I fall into the intertwine

The communion of bliss
As we finally kiss
And I come to see

The Heaven
Within you and me

Consciousness
Is just our true nature
Rising to the surface

The mind is a diamond
A key, pointed and clear
Like an arrow of clarity

As we live in duality
Our breath is the portal
The heart is the doorway
To our cradle of Divinity

The jewelled heart is our epicentre
A constellation of life, death and rebirth
So we come to know the truth
Beckoning us

All is revealed
We were never alone

Just a flicker of energy
Over and over
The jewels in the light

Consciousness
Calling us home

We all have a key
We can all find the door
Just open your heart
And you will be
No more

Where can I feast
Not on food or wine

But on the love
That resides inside

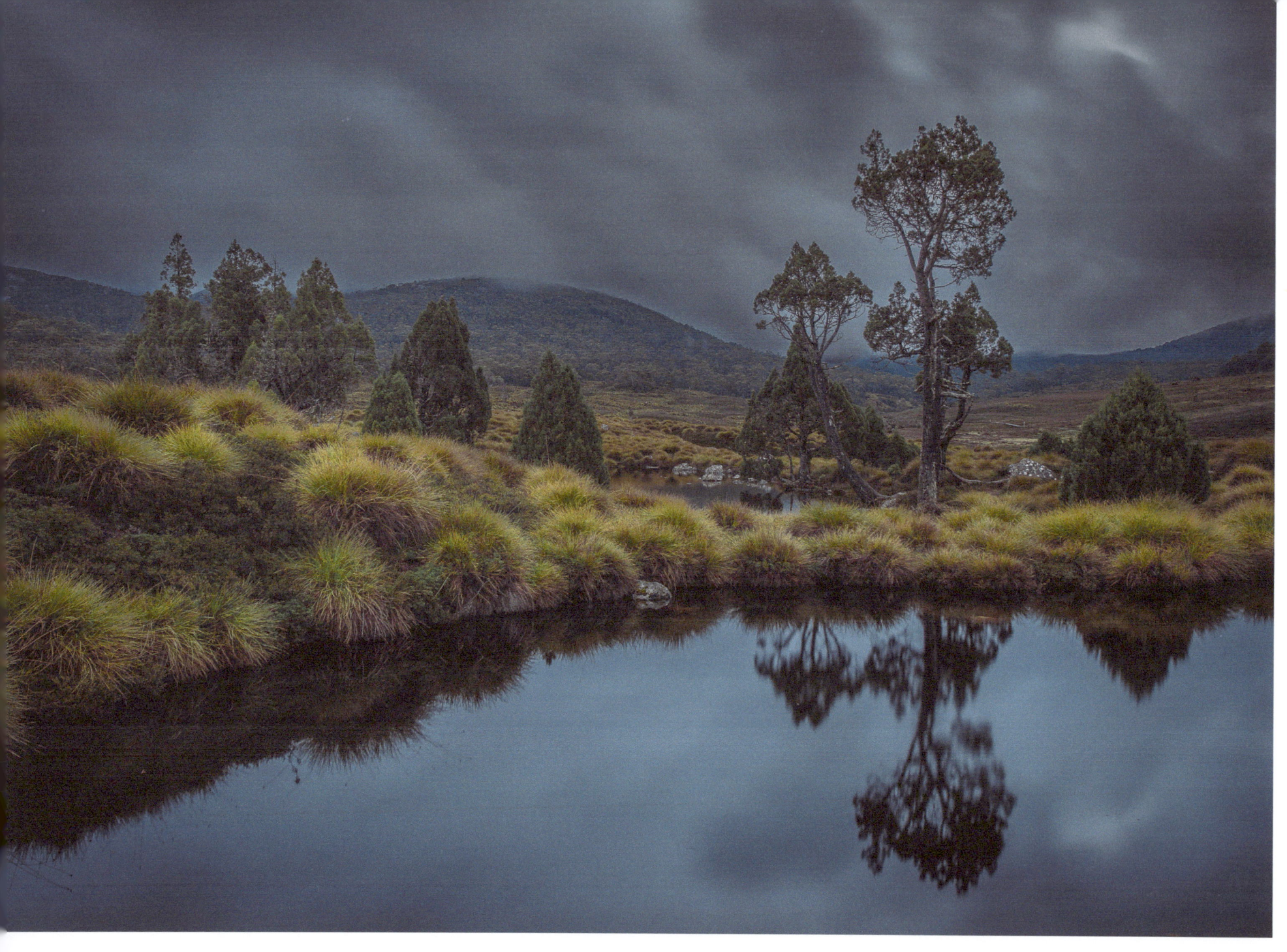

CRADLE MOUNTAIN NATIONAL PARK

When I come to the ocean
And finally feel you

My heart resonates
With our ballad of love
The symphony of you

All my pain dissolves
All my suffering ceases
And all that remains

Is a beautiful pearl
A reflection of you

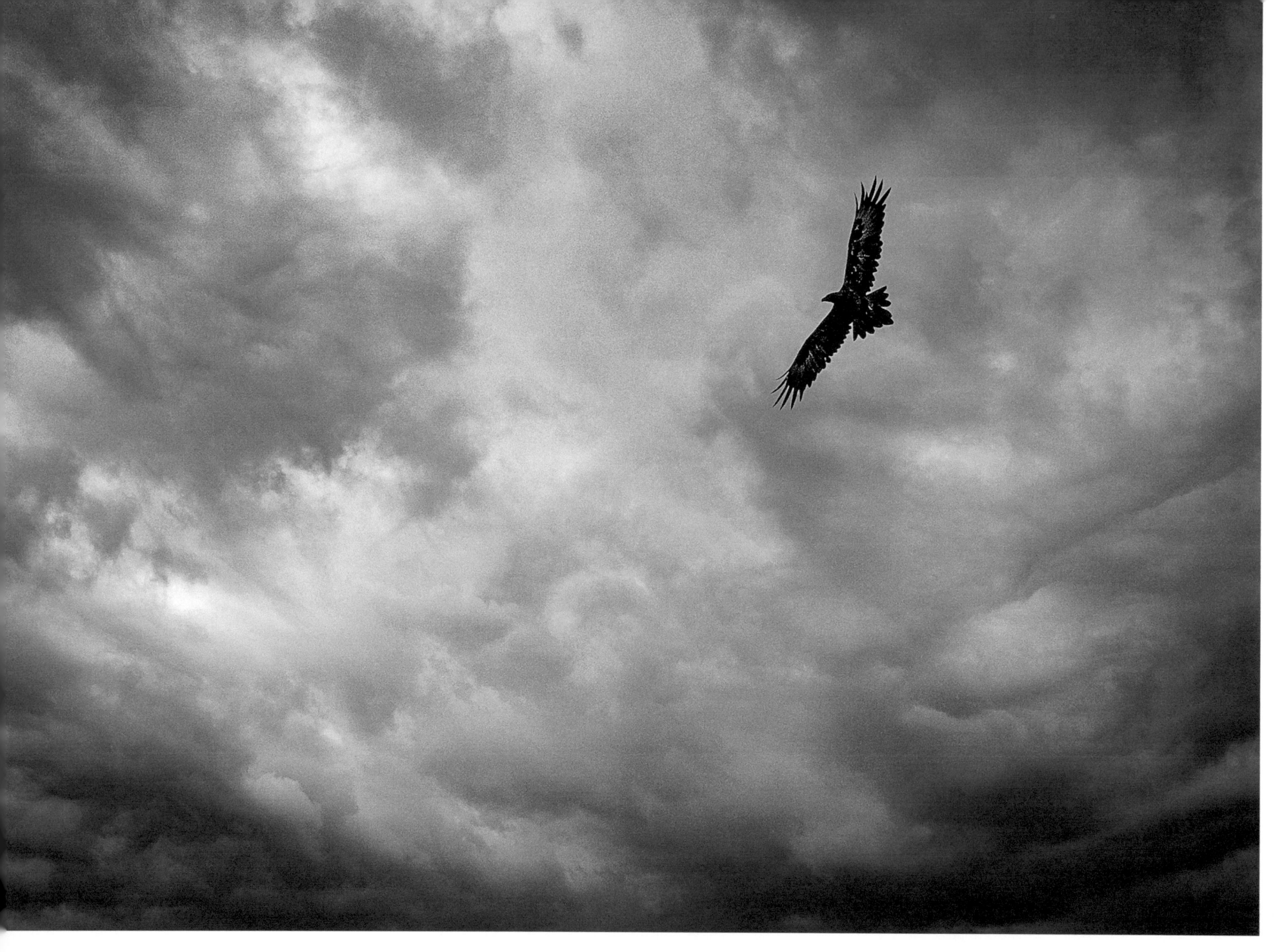

WEDGE-TAILED EAGLE, CORINNA

Like a hand on glass
It is in the shadow
That I finally see you

For you are not the hand
The glass or the pane

But tentacles of light
An interplay
A dance
Between the shadow
And the flame

Duality is not only fire and ice
Summer and rain

Duality is remembering
How to see you again

So I may enter the abyss
To find my bliss

I no longer exist

As the truth appears clearly
Like stars in the sky

All that we are
Is beyond the sublime

All that we are
Exists beyond time

To break free
Harness your mind
Bow to your breath

We blossom, wither and die
Before we finally realise
How the sacred lives inside

Come be with me
Calls the Beloved

I will embrace you
Fill your cup with wine

Come take my hand
Sink into the ocean
Let your heart be free
Feel your soul singing to me

Who are we?
Just flesh and bone?

What is the Divine?
Just infinity beyond time?

Are we mortal flesh
Or just a moment in time?

What is impermanence
But a cycle of life, death, rebirth?

What is the cycle
But a flow of the Infinite?

What is the heart
But a seed of the Infinite?

What is the Infinite
But the shine in my heart?

When are we real?
When the flow awakens and shines across the eons

Then we are not just a moment in time
Then we are not just flesh and bone
Peeling and decaying

We are part of the infinitesimal flow
The seed lies in our heart
Waiting to ignite

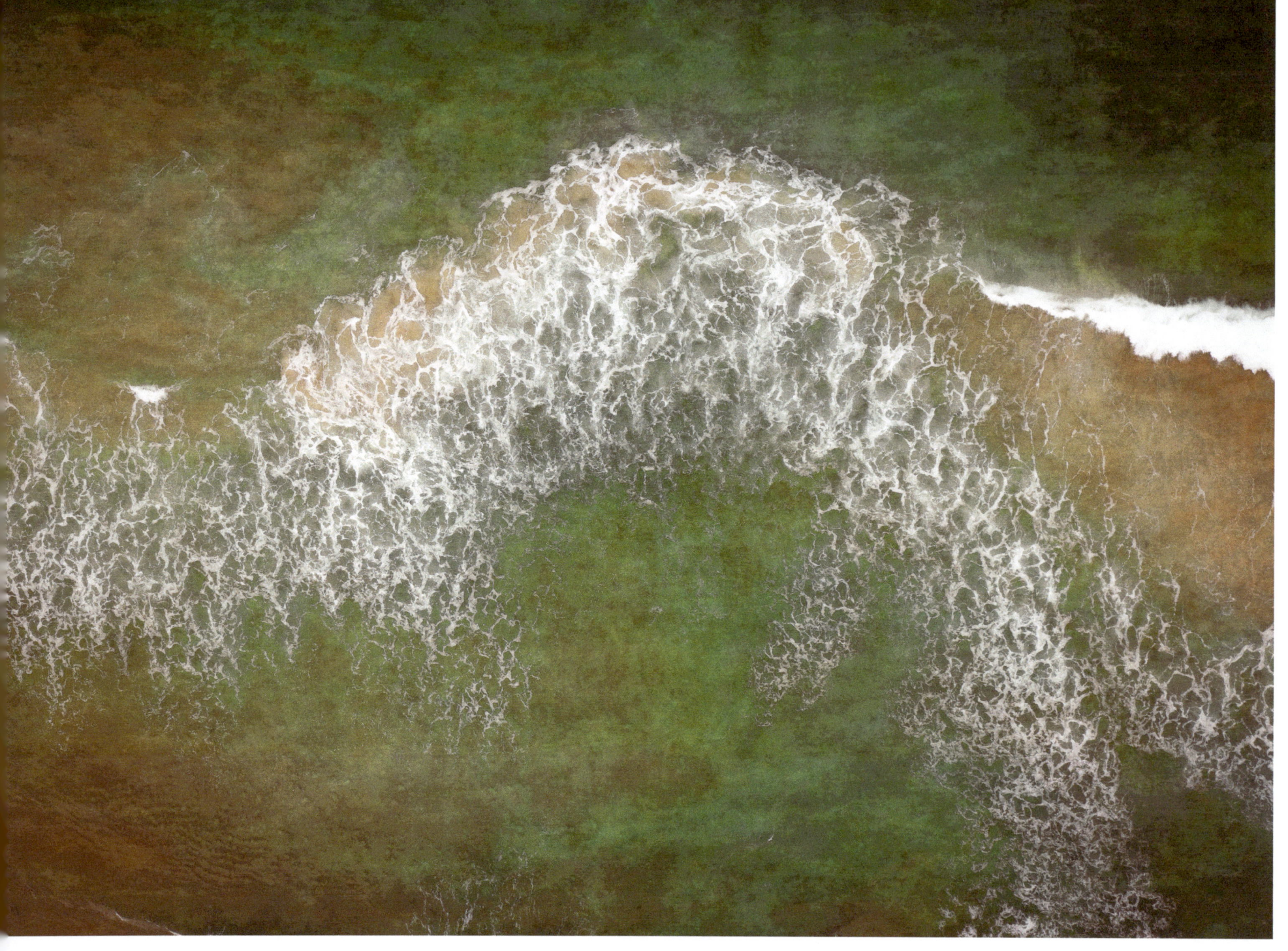

BINALONG BAY

When you are part of the Infinite Flow
All that dies is not real
And all that is real does not die

Love is the beginning
Love is the end
All between
Is only an illusion

Who are we
If not part of the Divine?

Are we bone and flesh?
Heart and mind?

Are we all of these?
Or just a moment?

A frequency of light
A breath away from home

Create peace in your life
Like a reflection, to see

The Beloved
Who lives within
You and me

Hold my hand
I will comfort you

Look into my eyes
Feel my presence

Let our hearts caress each other
Let our breath share the flow

If you just let go
So we share the space

You will feel
My utter embrace

How will we dream
When there are no birds in the sky?
How will we breathe
When the air is choked by dust?
What will we eat
When there are no fish in the sea?
Where will we walk
When the earth crumbles underneath?

Pray, who will we be
When all there is to see
Is shadow and misery?

As we sit on our throne of currency
And blood runs as far
As the eye can see

Our heart in despair
And our form
As hollow as can be

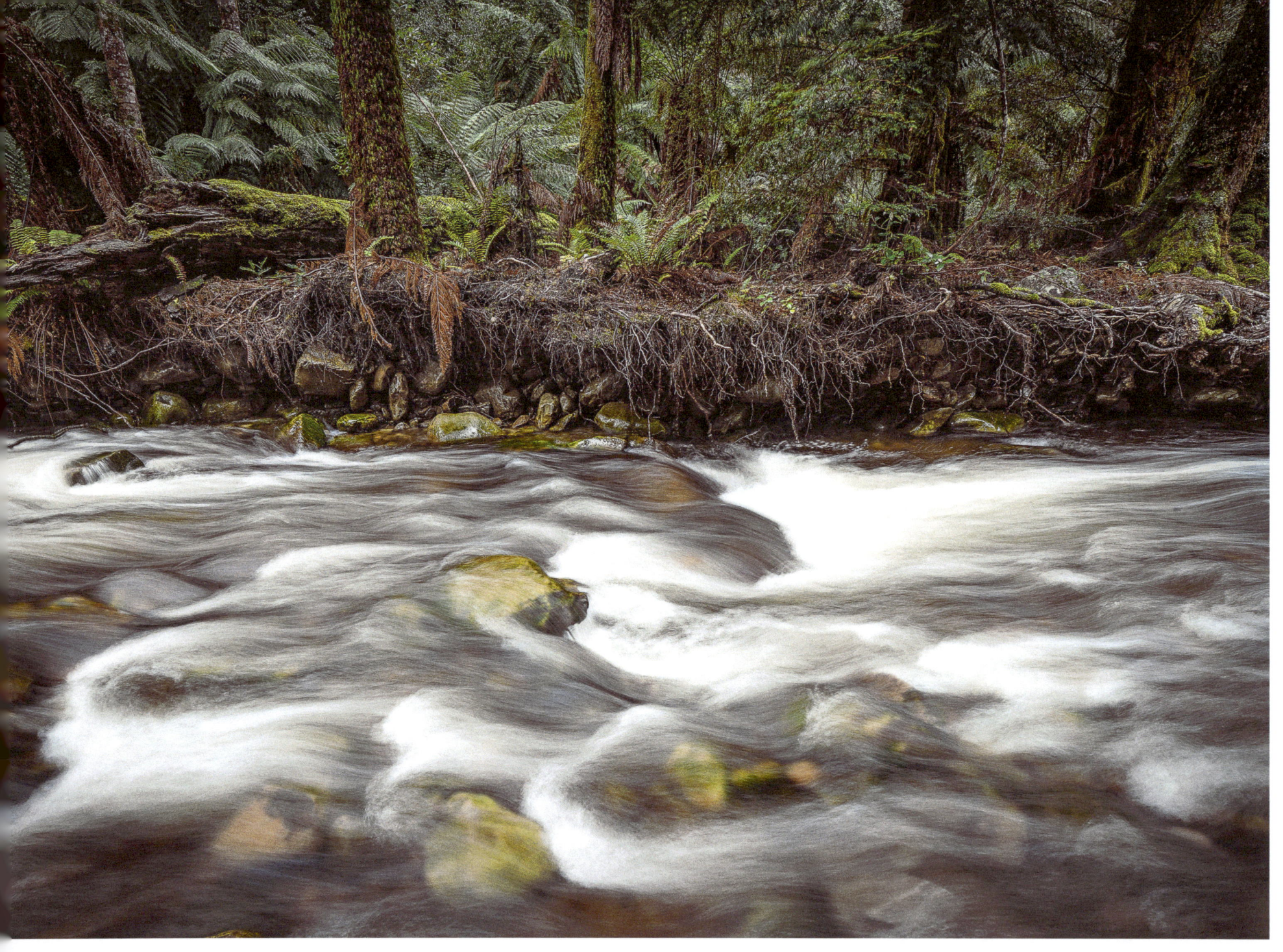

LIFFEY RIVER

Let your heart bleed
Not from loss

But of the love

Which speaks
Between you and me

Beloved

My heart overflows and bleeds for you
Love coming through, within the stillness of you

May all feel your presence, may all suffering cease

May my heart overflow, giving to others
The true love, inherent in you

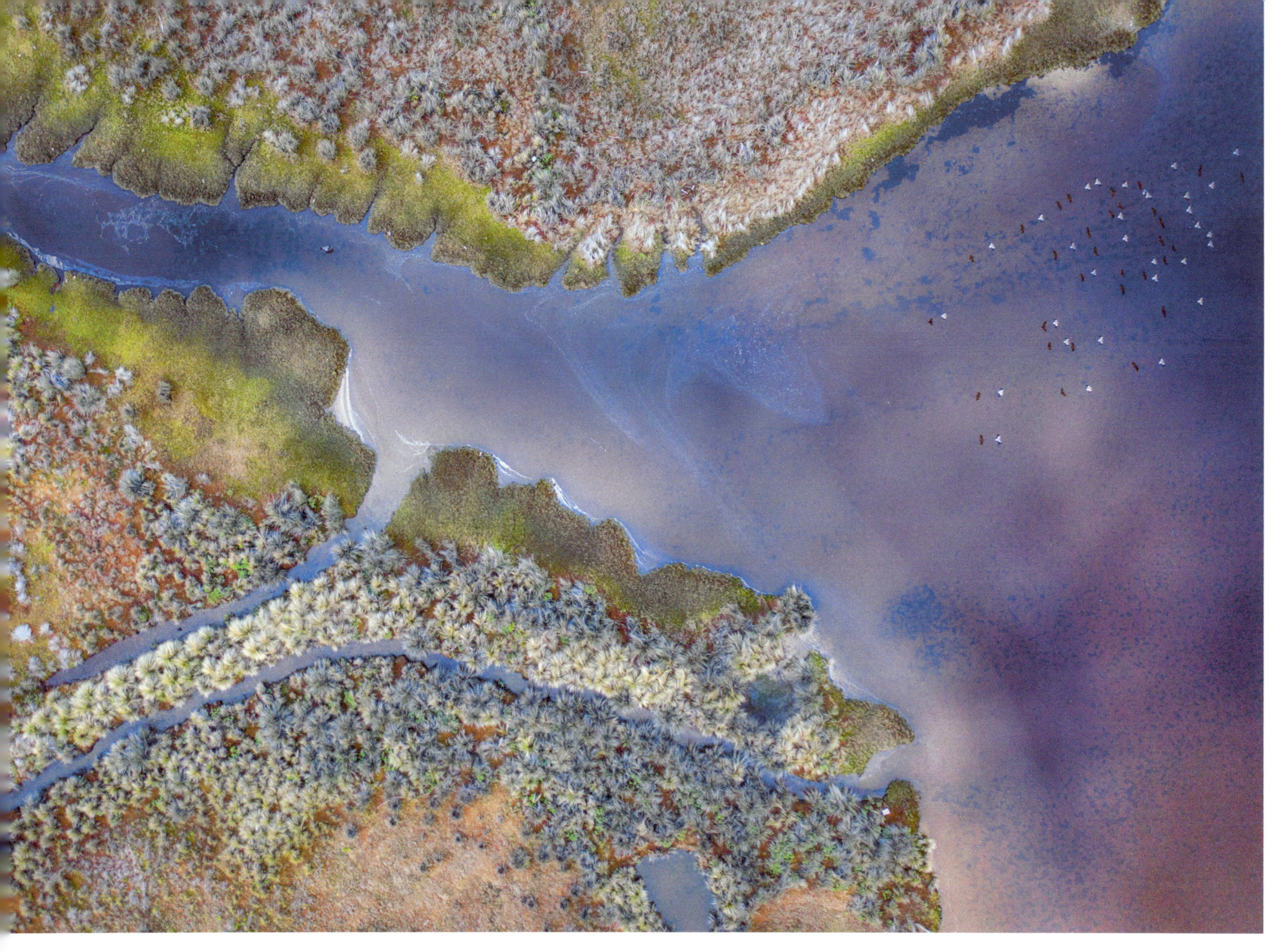
CYGNET WETLANDS

I fall to my knees
I let love take its hold

The truth lies within
We are a sacred vibration

Our interior light, the stars in our heart
Their spark of Divinity, so clear and true

Mapping the path, straight back to you

Let love be your anchor
Hold me close
As I learn how to make myself whole

Let me feel your flame
Take me past this world of pain

Even within joy
All of suffering is told
The love I hold so deep for others
Only takes a moment to unfold

Nothing is permanent
We cannot cling to the past
We cannot attach to those we love
We cannot hold tight to make it last

This is the kernel of truth, a ripening of hope
The only way through is to bow at your feet
Feel the love in my heart, as we finally meet

For I am no longer a rivet, a lock or a key
As I dive into the pool of my own Divinity
Take my hand, let me be with you
Let me understand all that I am

For the ultimate truth
The path to forever
Lives in your heart
Resplendent and true
My lotus flower sparks
Within you

There are many paths to the Divine
Many ways to enter the flow.

But to open the final door
It is the heart
We must know

Consciousness is the lotus flower
Settling in your mind

Consciousness is the sweet syrup
In the heart
Of the Divine

Death is the frequency of One
Death is only dissolution
To the great beyond

Death is within the intertwine

Death is what we do
As we dissolve
Completely into you

We never know when it's time to go
When it's time to say goodbye

But one thing is for sure
We will meet again
In the luminous space
Beyond the earth and the sky

As we sail the river of Life
Our mind is the rudder
Our breath is the wind
Our compass, the heart
Carrying us home

There is a stillness
And a presence
In coming to be

Take my hand
I will show you

Together
We will see

Rock me in the cradle
Awaken me from sleep

Ignite my seed
I am yours to keep

My heart held in your hands
No longer a seed
But a beautiful flower

Radiant and alive
Awakened and free

As I feel myself
Coming to be

The Divinity of you
Loving me

God is in the heart and soul of every being.
And when you open within yourself the secret temple in your heart,
then with the all-knowing intuition of the soul you shall read the book of life.
Then, and only then, will you contact the living God.
And you will feel [God] as the very essence of your being.

— Paramahansa Yogananda, *In the Sanctuary of the Soul: A Guide to Effective Prayer*

Lord
Make me an instrument of your peace

Where there is hatred
Let me sow love
Where there is injury
Pardon
Where there is doubt
Faith
Where there is despair
Hope
Where there is darkness
Light
Where there is sadness
Joy

Oh Divine Master
Grant that I may not so much seek to be consoled
As to console
To be understood
As to understand
To be loved
As to love

For it is in giving
That we receive
It is in pardoning
That we are pardoned
And it is in dying
That we are born to eternal life.

– St Francis of Assisi

With love…

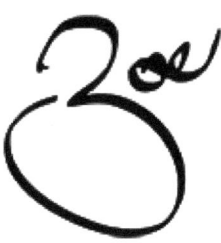

Interactive Press
an imprint of Interactive Publications
Treetop Studio • 9 Kuhler Court
Carindale, Queensland, Australia 4152
sales@ipoz.biz
https://ipoz.biz

First published by Interactive Press, 2025
© Zoe Leavitt (text)
© Craig George (photographs)
© David P Reiter (book design)

The moral rights of the creators have been asserted.

© 2025. All rights reserved. Without limiting the rights under copyright reserved above, no part of this publication may be reproduced, stored in or introduced into a retrieval system, or transmitted, in any form or by any means (electronic, mechanical, photocopying, recording or otherwise), without the prior written permission of the copyright owners and the publisher of this book.

ISBN 9781923435186 (PB); 9781923435193 (eBook)

 A catalogue record for this book is available from the National Library of Australia

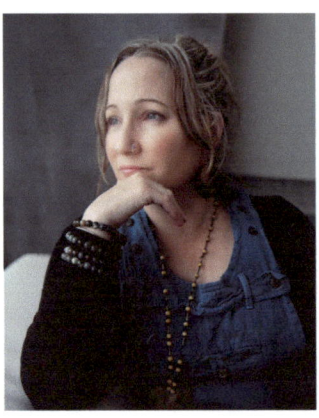

Zoe Leavitt is a writer and a psychologist. This anthology of poetry has been developed through a period of marked spiritual exploration and practice. An accomplished therapist for the past 26 years, Zoe is accustomed to working within the inner space of others. She believes our inner worlds are so much a part of who we are, yet rarely are they spoken of, or given enough attention to.

Zoe endeavours to invite you inward, to settle in your space of inner connection and to also perhaps, help illuminate a path of reflection and transcendence.

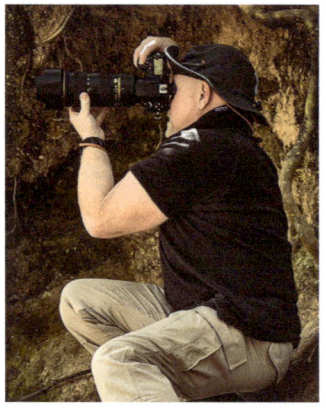

Craig George, husband of Zoe, has carved an impressive path through an array of professions. In a 30-year career with Victoria Police, he mastered and taught the art of surveillance photography. He's now an editorial photographer for the Launceston *Examiner* and his relocation to Tasmania in 2017 ignited a powerful creative renaissance, fuelled by the island's awe-inspiring natural landscapes. Craig has exhibited his work internationally, including in St. Petersburg, Russia. He was AIPP Victorian Professional Landscape Photographer of the Year (2016) and awarded the "Master of Photography" accreditation in 2018.

Many images in this book were captured during a 2018 expedition to the pristine Tarkine rainforest. A collection was later showcased in a University of Tasmania exhibition inaugurated by former Greens Leader and environmental activist Dr Bob Brown. View Craig's work at www.theraw-image.com or on Instagram at @the_raw_image.